MOTHERHOOD MINUTES

A 60-Day Devotional for Busy Moms

Eunice Ho

Motherhood Minutes: A 60-Day Devotional for Busy Moms

Printed in the United States of America

Cover art by Jeremy Ho
Edited by Christopher Ho
Author photograph by David Massey, © 2022

First edition: February 2023
Revised edition: March 2023

ISBN 978-1-7361060-3-7 (paperback)
ISBN 978-1-7361060-4-4 (ebook)

DEDICATION

I am dedicating this book to our parents:
Kim Soon Kyum & Kim Sun Seon and Ho Minsun & Ho Younhee.

Thank you for teaching us how to love God and be faithful to Him in every season and circumstance. Without the love and sacrifices you have all made for us, our family would not be where we are today. Thank you for the generational blessings you have passed on to us. We love you all and are deeply grateful to have you each as our parents.

이 책을 친정 부모님이신 Kim Soon Kyum/Kim Sun Seon 님,
그리고, 시부모님이신 Ho Minsun/Ho Younhee 님께 바칩니다.

모든 처한 환경에서 하나님을 사랑하고 그분을 신뢰할 수 있도록 가르쳐 주심에 감사드립니다.
우리를 향한 부모님의 사랑과 헌신이 아니였다면, 오늘 우리가 서 있는 이 곳에 있지 못했을 것입니다.
그리고, 대대로 물려주신 은혜와 축복에 감사 드리며, 진심으로 사랑합니다.
당신들께서 저희 부모님이심에, 마음 속 깊은 곳으로부터 깊은 감사의 마음을 전합니다.

ACKNOWLEDGEMENTS

Thank you God for this beautiful life you have given me.

To my love, Chris: Thank you for creating space for me to write over these months and for your patience in editing and your attention to details that I often miss. You are my best friend and my greatest supporter. Thank you for always helping me organize my dreams so that they can actually come to pass!

To my five wonderful blessings: Jonathan, Jeremy, Zach, Abby, and Joy. I love being your mom! Thank you for always loving, supporting, and encouraging me. I look forward to seeing the journey where God leads each one of you in your lives.

Jeremy, thank you for the many hours you spent drawing this beautiful book cover. Since mom and dad can only draw stick figures, I know without a doubt that your artistic gift is straight from God. May you continue to partner with Him in sharing your art with the world.

Thank you to all of our faithful supporters of The Journey Home Ministries. I would not have been able to write this book without your prayers and financial support. I am eternally grateful that you generously sow into our ministry.

Thank you John and Min Suh for translating my dedication into Korean.

CONTENTS

Title Page
Copyright
Dedication
Acknowledgements
Preface
Introduction
Day 1 1
Day 2 3
Day 3 5
Day 4 8
Day 5 11
Day 6 13
Day 7 15
Day 8 18
Day 9 21
Day 10 23
Day 11 26
Day 12 28
Day 13 31
Day 14 33
Day 15 35

Day 16	38
Day 17	40
Day 18	42
Day 19	44
Day 20	46
Day 21	49
Day 22	52
Day 23	54
Day 24	56
Day 25	58
Day 26	60
Day 27	62
Day 28	65
Day 29	68
Day 30	70
Day 31	72
Day 32	74
Day 33	76
Day 34	78
Day 35	80
Day 36	82
Day 37	84
Day 38	86
Day 39	88
Day 40	90
Day 41	94
Day 42	97
Day 43	99

Day 44 101
Day 45 103
Day 46 105
Day 47 107
Day 48 109
Day 49 111
Day 50 113
Day 51 115
Day 52 117
Day 53 120
Day 54 123
Day 55 125
Day 56 127
Day 57 129
Day 58 131
Day 59 133
Day 60 135
About the Author 137

PREFACE

Hey friends! My name is Eunice. I am a wife to my amazing husband Chris and we have been married for twenty-one years. I am a mother to five wonderful children. I have three boys and two girls, ages twenty, eighteen, seventeen, fifteen, and ten. I am deeply grateful for my beautiful blessings, but if I am honest, motherhood began as a very bumpy journey. I got pregnant with my first son right after our honeymoon, and although we were open to having kids right away, Chris and I had no clue what raising kids entailed. I love that I was able to have my kids when I was young (I was twenty-three when I had my first son), but I feel like I was put on a fast track to motherhood. I had very little experience with children because I was the youngest child in my family. I was never much of a "kid person" so I never babysat much before I had my first baby.

I have learned so many things on this journey of motherhood, mostly through trial and error. I am deeply grateful to God for His blood that covers over our sins, and for the gift of forgiveness when we repent. I am not a perfect parent, and I am thankful for the lessons God taught me while raising my kids. I am grateful that when I say sorry to my kids, they forgive me and we grow closer in relationship instead of further from each other.

Now that my three boys are almost all adult ages, I would love to help encourage and inspire any moms out there that are looking for guidance through the years of raising kids. Even with all my many imperfections, I absolutely love being a mom and I love the relationships we can foster with our kids if we are willing to allow the Lord to stretch and shape us.

People often ask me how I survived having four children in five years. I laugh because I honestly can't remember it all! I was very sleep deprived and like some of you, I didn't have my family close by to help me with babysitting. This was challenging at times, but I knew that God loves children and according to the Bible, children are a blessing, so I just kept looking forward to the future. If you only look at your present circumstances, changing a gazillion diapers a day, cooking and feeding kids over and over again, cleaning up after their messes, and not sleeping enough for several months or years, you will miss out on a blessing. Often the best things in life take the most work and effort. Deep in my heart I knew that although things were hard and we were often in survival mode, there was something great the Lord was building in my life.

I love learning from older, wiser people. I want to gain understanding from godly people who have walked before me. When I was a young mom, a common question I would ask the older moms at our church (the ones who already had adult children) was, "Are you glad that you had the number of kids that you did, or do you wish you had more? What would you tell your younger self?" Unanimously, the moms would say, "I wish I had one or two or three more children. Of course it was hard when they were babies and toddlers, but now that they are old, I really wish I had been willing to have more kids." It always stuck in my heart and my head when those moms would say that to me. I love having a larger family and although it was very challenging at times when they were young – truthfully I had many hard days, some days ending in tears, some days ending in eating lots of chocolate as soon as the kids were in bed – it was worth everything to have these five blessings in my life.

When I was a young mom, I wanted to know the right formula to do everything. This drove me, my husband, and probably the people around me, crazy. As I have grown in the

Lord and as a person, I realize that life is indeed a journey. And I can do my very best at parenting, but I am a frail human with great weaknesses. Despite my best efforts, there will likely come a day when my kids might need some counseling from their childhood from having me as their parent, and that is fine with me. I am not God. I am not perfect. But God gave me to my kids as their mom, and that means He entrusted me with their lives and as long as I am giving my all, He will be faithful in filling in the gaps of my inadequacies. That is why we need God.

If you are reading this book and you do not know Jesus as your Lord and Savior, I invite you to say this prayer with me:

Dear Heavenly Father,
Please forgive me for my sins. I am sorry for (list your sins here that come to mind right now). I ask that You come into my heart and set me free from sin. Thank You for dying on the cross for my sins and thank You for rising again. I invite You to be Lord over every area of my life.
In Jesus' name, Amen.

If you prayed this prayer, I encourage you to find a solid, life-giving local church to plug into where you can grow in your relationship with God.

I really believe that God needs to be the foundation for us to have a healthy family. I am excited to share what God has taught me about motherhood over these twenty years of being a mom. Thank you so much for joining me for my Motherhood Minutes devotional!

INTRODUCTION

I want to share a story with you that was pivotal in my journey of motherhood. It was extremely painful at the time, but grew and matured me in countless ways that I am so grateful for. I believe that almost every mom can relate to my story to some degree.

When my boys were four, three, and two years old, Chris and I drove halfway across the country to attend a series of meetings that my husband was invited to participate in. We were super excited to attend this event, so the seventeen hours of driving with three small children didn't bother us much. Chris and I are always down for a good road trip. Chris had to leave early on the second day of meetings since he would be actively involved in the event that day. I arrived a few hours later with my three boys and sat in the back of the sanctuary. I had great hopes that I could keep them quiet long enough so that I could listen to the message.

After just a few minutes of the sermon, my sons began making some noise. I was so engaged in the message that I honestly didn't notice, or maybe it's because I was so used to their noise that I didn't pay attention to their sounds. Well, suddenly an usher stood in front of me with a very sour look on his face. He very rudely asked me and the kids to leave the meeting.

Everyone in the surrounding pews turned and stared at us. I was horrified and felt so humiliated, but of course I obliged.

I quickly rushed out of the sanctuary into the entryway of the building only to find that there was no other space for me to take the kids to keep them quiet, except the women's bathroom! I led the kids into the bathroom, fighting back my tears of disappointment and humiliation, and tried to keep them as quiet as possible until the meeting was over. After about thirty minutes, when I heard a commotion in the entryway, I realized the service was over and I emerged out of the bathroom with my three boys and found Chris.

Literally everyone who came out of the sanctuary was raving about how amazing the service was, including Chris. At this point he had no clue why I was sitting in the bathroom with the boys because he was asked to stay in the front for the whole meeting. Meanwhile, I felt absolutely horrible inside but was still trying to hold it together for the rest of the events that day. Not only was I feeling sad and humiliated, but now I was also deeply disappointed that I completely missed the service where others said they encountered God!

At the end of the night, a sweet older mom friend walked up to me and asked, "Are you ok?" I quickly nodded yes, in hopes that she would leave me alone. However, in her wisdom she said, "Really? Because you haven't looked ok all day..." At that point, I just burst into tears and sobbed my heart out to her. I explained what happened and about how disappointed I was that in a community where people preach about how children are a gift from God, how could I be so rudely kicked out of the service because of a little noise from my kids? And did I mention that we drove seventeen hours just to attend these meetings?

This kind and seasoned mother of seven, just listened to me, let me cry, and told me that she was very sorry. I was so grateful for the compassion of this older woman. But God used this challenging incident to launch me into a journey of healing, where He was trying to heal these broken places in my heart. I ended up crying the whole next week after those meetings. I was deeply hurt and places of pain in my heart were being exposed. I would literally wake up in the middle of the night that week and my face and pillow were wet because I was actually crying, **in my SLEEP**!

When I was single, I was active in ministry and was a leader in our church, so naturally I was very visible and present in every meeting. But after I got married and had a honeymoon baby, my priorities changed as my season of life shifted. On the weeks when my husband would preach, I would stay in the back of the sanctuary with my son, and sometimes would have to leave the room to sit behind the glass doors so that his noise wouldn't be a distraction. Our church didn't have the technology back then to have a cry room where you could hear the sermon while you were watching your baby in the back. I felt so spiritually dull, but I thought this was normal. This caused some deep sadness and disappointment in my heart that I ignored with the busyness of the season. I realized that I never fully surrendered this sadness and disappointment to the Lord until this incident and that is what led to my weeklong tear bath.

I finally could not stuff my disappointments in any longer, but more importantly, God didn't want me to hold onto those things any longer. **This painful incident actually was a blessing!** Because after I forgave the usher and saw what God was trying to bring up so that I could deal with it, there was genuine healing for me. This incident caused me to face my pain, heal, mature, and embrace my season of young motherhood.

Up until that point, I had passively accepted caring for my sweet babies and the changes this new chapter brought, but I had not embraced it for all that God had intended it to be. Once I embraced the season of motherhood that God had me in, He gave me great joy in it. I grew to love being a mom. It is a great privilege and I feel honored that I have been an involved mother to my children.

In my immaturity, when I became a mom, I did not fully grasp that **God is completely able to meet me anywhere**. He can meet me at a church service with the best of preachers, He can meet me at a revival meeting, He can meet me in a prayer meeting, but He can also meet me in the kitchen when I am doing dishes for the thousandth time, He can meet me during the day when I am homeschooling my kids, He can meet me when my kids are sick and my husband is away on a trip and I am wiping my four-year-old's nose for the twentieth time, and He can also meet me in the bathroom (like he did when I was twenty-eight), when I had nowhere else to hide. When I was feeling humiliated and sad, God met me.

I hope that this devotional helps you connect with God in your everyday, normal minutes of life as a busy mom. I am writing this book from my heart, from the moments that God has encountered me in my very ordinary, mundane life. Over the years, God continually showed me that I don't need a prayer room to meet with Him (although that is nice), I don't need prolonged periods of silence for Him to speak (although this could be helpful as well). He speaks to me while I am preparing dinner, chauffeuring my kids around town, doing laundry, and cleaning the counters of our kitchen. If we commune with Him throughout our ordinary day and lean in to His voice, He is so faithful in meeting with us.

1 John 4:19 says, "We love because he first loved us." If you are in that place of feeling dry or distant from the Lord like I did when I was a young mom, I encourage you to reach out into His loving arms. He is waiting to connect with you sweet momma. I pray that you will embrace Him because He is already there, waiting for you. Or if you are in a place of just desiring more inspiration on your motherhood journey, I am excited that you picked up this book. I hope that you will enjoy these devotionals for the next sixty days!

DAY 1

Make Your Home in Me

This is what the Lord says: "Heaven is my throne, and the earth is my footstool. Where is the house you will build for me? Where will my resting place be?"

ISAIAH 66:1

Have you ever heard someone say, "This is my life verse..." and then they share some cool scripture? I always thought that was a good concept, but never felt an affinity to one particular verse. But over the years that I have been walking with the Lord, and especially as I became a wife and mom, I have come to realize the scripture above is my life verse and encapsulates the desire of my heart.

I want the Lord to find His habitation in me and my home. Lord, here in my heart, among my family, will You find a welcoming place where You can dwell? As I was thinking of this scripture a few months ago, I felt like something new was highlighted to me. When I was young, I used to read this verse and think, "Of course the earth is described as God's 'footstool' because we are lowly and beneath Him; we are inferior; we are

His servants." But as I have grown and have more understanding about the Lord being a good, kind Father, I felt like He spoke this to me:

"Where do people usually rest their feet? When you go to someone's home who is the President, or your boss, or a new acquaintance, or someone you aren't fully comfortable with, would you enter into their home and just sit down and put your feet up? Isn't putting your feet up in host's home a sign of the comfort level you have with that person? If you feel welcomed, loved, and familiar in their home, that is when a person feels comfortable to put their feet up."

Moms, I encourage you to ask the Lord to rest and dwell in your heart and your home. This is a crucial step in us establishing families centered around Jesus. This verse is the cry of my heart, to be a resting place for my Father all the days of my life. May He look upon me and see someone from whom He can receive love, comfort, adoration; a place where He can truly rest and feel completely at home.

I invite you to pray this prayer today:

Dear Heavenly Father,

I surrender my life to You again. I give You (fill in the blank of whatever comes to mind that you need to surrender today). Fill me today and let me trust You with all things. You are welcome in my home and my family. May You find a resting place here among us. In Jesus' name, Amen.

DAY 2

Mom Guilt

Because of the Lord's great love we are not consumed, for his compassions never fail. They are new every morning; great is your faithfulness.

LAMENTATIONS 3:22-23

As a parent, there are many times that we feel like failures. I think mom guilt is something that plagues most moms at some point in their journey. I certainly wrestled with it for so many years.

Every new mom: "Did I feed him/her the right food?"

Every homeschool mom: "Did I teach him/her enough today? Am I failing his/her education?!"

Every mom: "Did I give them too much screen time today? Have they had too much junk food? Have I accomplished ANYTHING today?"

Having kids is a refining fire like no other. It reveals every selfish and weak place in our hearts. The truth is that we fail at times, but the good news is that when we repent and ask the Lord for forgiveness, and repent to our kids when needed, the

Lord extends His forgiveness to us. There's something about the morning, the sun reappearing, and the clouds making the sky beautiful that feels like a fresh start, a new beginning. Are you going to let yesterday's failures plague you today? If God has forgiven you, why can't you forgive yourself and start afresh?

Satan wants to keep us in this trap of guilt and shame. My mom guilt never helped me become a better mom. Once I gave all that mom guilt and my many failures to God, that's when I became a better mom. I became more relaxed, less fearful, and had more faith and dependence on God.

One day when I was feeling guilty about my lack as a mom, the Lord spoke this to me: "If you give Me your best, I will be faithful to fill in the gaps for your children." I have clung to this word for years and I give this word to you, precious momma. If you give God your best in raising your kids, trust that He will fill the gaps of your inadequacies.

I invite you to pray this prayer today:

Dear Heavenly Father,
Please forgive me for these ways that I have sinned (name any sins that may come to mind). I give You my kids again and I ask that You fill in the gaps for where I fall short. Thank You for Your mercy!
In Jesus' name, Amen.

DAY 3

Are Children a Blessing?

Children are a heritage from the Lord, offspring a reward from him. Like arrows in the hands of a warrior are children born in one's youth. Blessed is the man whose quiver is full of them. They will not be put to shame when they contend with their opponents in court.

PSALM 127:3-5

One time when I was a young mom, doing the daily mundane things of life (changing diapers, making meals, feeding the kids, giving them a bath, putting them to bed, cleaning up their toys) the Lord spoke to my heart, "The world needs your children."

I was like, "Huh, that's a random thought. What does that mean Lord? Why does the world need my children? The world needs my children because they are cute? Is that what you mean?" My thinking was very shallow at the time because I was sleep deprived and a bit numb from the ordinariness of my life.

God unpacked this idea further to me that the world needs my kids because there are so many broken families in this world. The world needs our homes and lives to shine in the great darkness. I don't mean that we need meticulous homes where everything is sparkling clean and the children are perfectly behaved. I mean that God is raising up homes where God is first and parents and kids are committed to loving each other in the ways of the Lord.

When my husband and I were still single, and before we had even met, the Lord convicted each of us separately about how the world does not love and value children the way the Lord does, and how that mentality has crept into the church. The verse above, and many others, clearly indicate that children are a blessing. We had to confess and repent of our agreement with wrong beliefs regarding children. We had no idea then that the Lord was preparing us for our future marriage and large family!

We have been blessed to live in several communities that valued children and large families, but we have also experienced the opposite. I remember one time we went out to eat at a fast-food restaurant at a nearby mall when we had our three little boys. A lady sitting at a nearby table looked at us, and disdainfully said, "Why on earth would you do that to yourselves?" We have heard many other comments like this through the years. Or, we will hear another parent talk about how their children are horrible or ruined their life – right in front of their children!

I know parenting is hard, and truth be told, there are certainly days when children do not feel like a blessing. But I'm not talking about a one-off comment or a bad day. I'm talking about a pervasive mentality that has crept into our society where children are viewed as a nuisance, an inconvenience, an obstacle to our goals, or something even worse.

Don't worry, we have also experienced a lot of positive remarks regarding our large family. When we lived in the Middle East, people found our family fascinating. Not only did they find it incredible that Chris was providing for five kids, but we even had a couple of men ask him if he had more than one wife. In some parts of that culture where polygamy was accepted, some men were amazed that Chris only had one wife and that I birthed all five of these children. When they found out that yes, all these children came from me, their response was always deep respect for me and some kind of congratulatory remark.

Moms, the world needs children who love God and love their neighbors. Children who know their worth because they know the One who created them and gives them dignity and value. Our children are meant to be a blessing to this world. If you recognize that you have allowed wrong mindsets regarding your children (or children in general) to influence you, let's repent and ask God to give us His heart and mind towards children.

I invite you to pray this prayer today:

Dear Heavenly Father,
Forgive me for any way I have adopted a worldly mindset regarding children. Help me to see them the way You do. Jesus, please be the center of our families. Help me to love You and please help me to teach my kids how to love You every day.
In Jesus' name, Amen.

DAY 4

God's Provision

Therefore I tell you, do not worry about your life, what you will eat or drink; or about your body, what you will wear. Is not life more than food, and the body more than clothes? Look at the birds of the air; they do not sow or reap or store away in barns, and yet your heavenly Father feeds them. Are you not much more valuable than they? Can any one of you by worrying add a single hour to your life?

MATTHEW 6:25-27

We got married in our early twenties, while Chris was a student at Princeton Theological Seminary. We were so broke. We had a honeymoon baby and I was quite morning sick when I got pregnant. I had a part-time job, but we were barely making ends meet.

After my husband graduated, he was offered a part-time position at our church. We loved our church and wanted to stay committed there, so he got another part-time job since we desperately needed the income. He looked for something where he could begin immediately and he found a job delivering pizzas. Thinking back, I am so proud of Chris, because even though this was not his dream job, he is very humble and hard-working. He was willing to do anything to provide for our little family.

We were living paycheck to paycheck when we had our first son, Jonathan. One day I realized that we only had a couple of diapers left for our son, but payday was sadly nowhere in sight. I remember I told Chris about our predicament and he said, "Well, we can't buy diapers yet because we only have enough money in our bank account for my gas that I need for work." We didn't know what to do. Maybe we prayed but I honestly don't remember.

Later that same day after this stressful conversation, we drove to a gas station to fill up Chris' tank with the gas he needed for his pizza deliveries that week. When we pulled up to the pump, the gas attendant looked at us and then randomly said to my husband,

"Do you need diapers?"

At first, we thought we misunderstood him. He did not wait for our response and started walking back to his office. Still confused, we watched the man come back out holding a pack of a nice brand of diapers IN MY SON'S EXACT DIAPER SIZE! He said, "Someone just left this here earlier today for some reason. Do you guys want them?" I mean seriously, my husband and I were in complete shock as we thanked him. We were just in absolute awe of God and His provision. How in the world did some random stranger leave a pack of brand-new diapers in my son's exact size at a gas station?!

Honestly, we have seen so many financial miracles in our lives, but this diaper story still gets my attention to this day. God knows each one of us. He knows our needs. He knows our desires. He loves my children more than I do. As a mother, it is hard for me sometimes to grasp that God loves my kids more than me, but it is true! I share this story to remind myself and anyone else reading about this truth. We are so loved and cared for by our Heavenly Father. He is so kind. It is a lesson that I am learning and relearning every day.

I invite you to pray this prayer today:

Dear Heavenly Father,
Thank You for Your great love for me and my family. I love You. Thank You for providing for all of my needs. (If you have a need, bring it before Him now.) I pray that I would see You working in my life today and every day.
In Jesus' name, Amen.

DAY 5

Discipling Our Kids

Love the Lord your God with all your heart and with all your soul and with all your strength. These commandments that I give you today are to be on your hearts. Impress them on your children. Talk about them when you sit at home and when you walk along the road, when you lie down and when you get up...be careful that you do not forget the Lord, who brought you out of Egypt, out of the land of slavery.

DEUTERONOMY 6:5-7, 12

People in the world may not know it yet, but they long for and need to see healthy, loving children that are raised in God-centered homes. Christ-centered homes where the parents put God first and love each other in humility. Homes where children are taught who God is, what He is like, and how He commands us to live. Homes where children can feel free to ask their parents about anything. All these lessons should be imparted to our kids throughout their lives, around the dining room or living room, over ice cream when we are just living our normal, ordinary lives.

As we can see in the passage above, the Israelites were told to not only learn the commandments of God, but to impress them on their children, and to talk about them in their homes and in everyday settings. This doesn't have to be done in a heavy-handed manner, but as parents we need to learn how to have these kinds of conversations with our kids. Childrens' and youth ministries are great, but I have seen too many parents expect their churches to do 100% of the work of teaching their children in the Lord, when in truth, the Lord expects us as parents to do the majority of it. Parents, I would encourage you to see yourselves as the primary disciplers of your children, and see your church's ministries and programs as a supplement.

My parents did a lot of things well, and they taught us to love and follow the Lord, but there were a lot of important topics that we never discussed, probably for a number of reasons. Maybe we can't teach our kids everything they will need to learn, but we should try our best to cover the most important topics, and they should feel like they can ask us about anything and we can have a good conversation about it, even difficult topics like sex, relationships, mental health, failures, fears, finances, etc.

If you have yet to have these types of discussions with your kids, I encourage you to begin today. It's never too late and today is a good day to start!

I invite you to pray this prayer today:

Dear Heavenly Father,
Thank You for my children. Please give me ideas in how to teach my kids about who You are. Give me divine wisdom and understanding. Help me to recognize the opportunities we have in everyday moments.
In Jesus' name, Amen.

DAY 6

Bearing Fruit

Let us not become weary in doing good, for at the proper time we will reap a harvest if we do not give up.

GALATIANS 6:9

Having small children can be busy and exhausting. I fully admit that when my kids were little, I was in complete survival mode. I was learning how to be a wife, a mom, to cook, to clean, to be a pastor's wife, and many more things. I was also pregnant or nursing for over ten years of my life. There were so many days (if not every day) that I honestly had to wonder, "What am I doing with my life? Is anything I am doing worth it? Am I making a difference in my kids' lives?" To all the moms with little ones, I want to encourage you, "Yes! What you are doing truly matters!"

The love, care, nurture, sacrifice, discipline, and security that you are instilling in your children is immeasurable. That's why the day to day can be so challenging. We cannot necessarily see the fruit or quantify it yet, but it's coming! When my kids were little, I used to think, "Lord, if I could just see some real fruit daily from my labors, I would know this is all worth it..." But that's the hard part. As a mom of littles, you often don't.

It was in this season of my life that the Lord encouraged my weary, sleep-deprived heart with the idea of a fruit tree. Some things I learned about fruit trees: a fruit tree takes two to five years to start bearing fruit. It takes multiple things for a fruit tree to grow and thrive: proper watering, sunlight, fertilizer, mulch, enough space to grow, pruning, and time! If it takes this much care in order to grow a simple fruit tree, how much more work will it take to help produce a healthy human being?

I know the daily tasks in life can seem boring and draining some days, but don't lose heart. Cooking another meal, nursing your infant again, kissing a child's scraped knee, reading another story, correcting them when they are being mean to a sibling – the list is endless. All of these things are nurturing their precious hearts, minds, and bodies and are so important for a person to thrive! I am blessed to see some fruit in each of my kids in this season of motherhood, and it's so encouraging. I am witnessing my beautiful children blossoming into some really awesome adults and I am so thankful that I didn't give up in my efforts when they were small.

Moms, the daily, mundane things that you are sowing into your families will indeed reap a beautiful harvest one day. Please receive this encouragement into your hearts and don't give up!

I invite you to pray this prayer today:

Dear Heavenly Father,
Thank You for Your great love for me and my kids. I pray that You would give me the vision to see that the seeds I am planting in my kids' lives today will produce good fruit in the future. Please give me fresh vision and faith to believe this.
In Jesus' name, Amen.

DAY 7

Draw Near

Come near to God and he will come near to you.

JAMES 4:8

I was constantly busy when all of my kids were little. Now that they are older, my life has ebbs and flows of busyness that look different than before. When they were little, it was all about feeding them, changing diapers, or breaking up toddler fights and tantrums. Now my busyness looks like shuttling them around town, talking them through different situations with friends or teachers, and cooking huge meals to feed six adult-sized bodies and one ten-year-old. Whatever my busyness looks like, over the years I have needed to find ways that have sustained me in keeping my connection to God.

I know some wise mothers who said that spending quiet time with the Lord in the early morning, before all the kiddos wake up, was an anchor in their lives. I actually do this now, but when I was younger I would get inspired after hearing them say this, and I would try to get up before the kids and repeatedly fail. And the times that I actually did miraculously awake before the kids and do my quiet time, I would have terrible days. I would be irritable and cranky the rest of the day to my husband and kids. Now that we are all older, getting up earlier than my kids is easy and having coffee in the morning while reading my Bible and praying is routine.

But when they were young, I needed to find ways to connect with God that were doable and didn't make me grumpy all day. I had to come to terms with the reality that what gives one mom life, was making me an irritable mom. I love sleep so much and the Bible actually says that "...he grants sleep to those he loves" (Psalm 127:2b). God loves me and I have a high value for sleep. Now, I have no shame about this being my reality.

Spending time with God is so critical for our well-being and our family's well-being. I had to figure out ways to spend with Him that actually work for me, not for someone else. Don't compare yourself to others in how you spend time with God. Find a rhythm or system that works realistically for your life.

How can I grow as a daughter of God if I am not staying connected to Him? And how can I ever teach my kids about God if I am not continuing to learn about Him? Find a way to pray throughout your day (like when you are doing dishes or cooking and the kids are occupied). Incorporate Bible reading and worship in your day (even if it means listening to the Bible on your phone while driving).

I am at a point in my life where I am just done with making excuses about not spending time with God. I have wasted too many years in the past doing this. I know that He longs to meet with each one of us. I really encourage you to keep searching for practical ways that help *you* connect with Him in your daily life.

I invite you to pray this prayer today:

Dear Heavenly Father,
Thank You for loving me and waiting for me. I want to meet with You today. Please come fill me up with Your presence and show me how to stay connected to You today and every day.

In Jesus' name, Amen.

DAY 8

Tears

You keep track of all my sorrows. You have collected all my tears in your bottle. You have recorded each one in your book.

PSALM 56:8 (NLT)

How do you view tears?

Because of my Korean culture and upbringing, I used to believe that tears were a clear sign of weakness. When I was growing up, I used to feel embarrassed for people who would cry in public (not young children of course, but basically anyone else). I was so uncomfortable around emotion, both mine and other people's.

Then in my mid-twenties I hit a wall with fear and other emotional junk in my life. I felt stuck and I didn't know how to overcome. One day a good friend suggested that I meet with her counselor. It was very expensive for our limited family budget, but my husband and I were able to plan and set aside money and time for me to go through this four-day intensive counseling. It was a huge sacrifice, but it was worth every penny.

The counseling was a crucial investment not only for my

emotional health, but also for the health of my marriage and family as well. One of the things that my counselor helped me identify was my blocked wall of emotions. Up until this point in my life, I basically gave myself permission to cry maybe once per year and almost always in the privacy of my own room where no one else was around. One key to breakthrough was when my counselor led me in a prayer to give my emotions to God. It was pretty disarming and vulnerable because I didn't know how my emotions would manifest and embarrass me. But this was a huge key in getting healed from the pain of my past.

God created emotions for a reason. God himself has emotions and we are created in His image. He does not apologize for having emotions, so why do we?

A year or so after I gave my emotions to God, my offering was tested. A woman that was in our church asked for a meeting with my husband and I. During the meeting she was sharing her frustrations about my husband and I as her leaders. She was really unhappy with us and said some pretty mean things. I am not one who tends to shy away from confrontation, and as she spoke, I started crying. I wasn't trying to run away from her words, I was still allowing her to talk and I was also able to talk, but I was shedding tears. Then in her frustration and discomfort with my tears, she said, "See! I can never bring anything up to you guys because then Eunice *always* starts crying..." (This was actually untrue as this woman would frequently request meetings with us and would always bring up a list of complaints that she wished she could change about our church, and I did not always cry as she stated.)

In that moment, I felt the Lord asking me, "Eunice, will you shut down your emotions again to appear strong to this woman? Or are you going to embrace the emotions that I gave you?"

I was tempted to shut down my tears, but instead I chose to embrace them. I told her, "I am sorry if my crying is making you uncomfortable, but this is honestly how I am processing what you are saying to us. My crying in front of you is a big step for me, but please feel free to still talk."

She left the meeting that night probably thinking I was quite weak and shortly after that left our church. But I was proud of myself because that was a defining moment for me. I chose to walk out my healing instead of putting on a façade again. Over the years, I have continued to let God work different things out in my life through my tears. And what I have found to be true many years later is that God has used my tears to heal me in places that I didn't even know needed healing. Now when I am sad or hurt, instead of stuffing down my sadness, I cry and release my pain. I usually feel so much better afterwards and I don't carry the baggage with me any longer. I often cry too when God is speaking to me and I am touched by His Spirit. He is doing something in my heart.

I admit that sometimes, I am still tempted to shut down my tears because of insecurity. But I now know that tears and emotions are not something to be afraid of or a sign of weakness. Allowing ourselves to feel our emotions and not stuffing them down is healthy and is actually a sign of strength.

I invite you to pray this prayer today:

Dear Heavenly Father,
I release all of my emotions into Your Lordship. Thank You for collecting all of my tears in a bottle. Thank You for giving me emotions. Thank You for caring about the things I care about. I pray that You would help me process my emotions in a healthy manner. Teach me Your ways and connect my heart to Yours.
In Jesus' name, Amen.

DAY 9

Soften Your Heart

Blessed is the one who always trembles before God,
but whoever hardens their heart falls into trouble.

PROVERBS 28:14

A young woman in her twenties once asked me a really good question: "How do I keep my heart from getting hard from disappointment and pain years down the line from now?" This was such a good question that it caused me to pause and really ponder my answer.

Life inevitably has disappointment, pain, trauma, loss, betrayal, and other unexpected things that can tempt anyone to harden their heart. But how does one position themself in a way so that they don't get calloused towards God and others? The only answer I could think of is this: take life one day at a time. Choose one day at a time to not harden your heart towards God and others, and that's how years down the line, we can ensure that we will still be teachable, pliable, and open to whatever God has for us.

Forgiving others for ways that we have been wronged by

them is a choice. Offering unjust circumstances up to God is also a choice. When things don't go the way that we planned for them to go, are we going to choose surrender or bitterness?

Some days, does your heart feel all mixed up like a puzzle? Like all the pieces from the box are clearly in front of you, but you simply cannot see the bigger picture? Perhaps this is making you feel distant from God? Marriage strife is at a high? Impatient with your kids? Having issues at work? Money problems pressuring you?

All these circumstances cause us to want to self-protect. But will you choose to surrender these things to God and trust Him again? Will you forgive those who have hurt you and release them?

Dear mom friends, let's not harden our hearts in self-preservation. The world has enough hard, skeptical, and cynical people. We are the people of God and can trust Him with our lives, circumstances, and futures. Give your burdens to God and choose to trust Him and to be open to others again.

I invite you to pray this prayer today:

Dear Heavenly Father,
Please forgive me for the ways I have hardened my heart towards You and others. I choose to forgive (fill in the blank with whomever God brings into your mind) and I release them into the freedom of my forgiveness. I choose to trust You with (speak out the burdens now that have been weighing on your heart). Thank You for being trustworthy. Please soften my heart to trust You and others again.
In Jesus' name, Amen.

DAY 10

His Loving-Kindness

Which of you, if your son asks for bread, will give him a stone? Or if he asks for a fish, will give him a snake? If you, then, though you are evil, know how to give good gifts to your children, how much more will your Father in heaven give good gifts to those who ask him!

MATTHEW 7:9-11

When you think of our Heavenly Father, what image pops into your head? Is He loving? Is He kind? Is He slow to anger? Is He abounding in love? Or is He harsh and mean? Is God an angry guy in the clouds that is ready to smite us at any moment when we do something wrong?

When I was in my early twenties, a dear mom mentor was praying over me and she said that she felt that I perceived God as a mean Father in heaven with a disciplining stick in His hand, demanding too much of me. When she said that, I felt sadly exposed, because the truth of her words stung and really opened my eyes to how I actually felt but wasn't willing to admit.

Over time, I began to realize that indeed I believed this lie that God is harsh and always makes me do things I don't want to do.

This lie actually guided a lot of my life's emotions and decisions.

In my late thirties, the Lord called our family to move overseas to the Middle East as missionaries. I was overwhelmed and angry when He first asked us to go. The nation we went to was very unstable and I was afraid.

I went "kicking and screaming" out of obedience to Him. But when we took this leap of faith, I was surprised because in my fear, God showed me His goodness, His compassion for a dying world, and His deep love for a people group that I barely had heard of before I boarded that plane. God also showed how much He loved me and my family. He revealed that He is the protector of my family, not me. He also showed me that He wanted me to live a life of freedom from anxiety. God delivered me from fear by bringing me to the deepest pit of despair, where our physical safety felt stripped from me. But in that pit, I offered to God my husband, my kids, and my whole life (again). In that time our good Father showed me that He would take care of us and the safest place in life is indeed in *His hands*, not mine.

Have you ever seen a toddler who is well loved look at their parent?

When they are having a peaceful moment, I see pure adoration for their parents in their eyes. We are their whole safe world and they adore us. If a child is looking at his/her parent like this, what parent in their right mind will not want to give them the whole world? My husband wants to give our children anything and everything that is good and wonderful and healthy for them, especially when they are looking at him with pure admiration! But as wonderful as he is, my husband is just a human father...How much more does our loving, amazing, rich, faithful, wise, all-powerful, merciful, just, and patient Heavenly Father want to give us good gifts?

Through the years, I have gained a tremendous measure of healing in many of areas in my life. As I have healed, my perception of God has thankfully transformed. I have begun to see His true, beautiful character more and more. I am thankful that God has revealed Himself as my good Father over and over again. He is not harsh, looking down on us waiting to discipline us for each mistake we make.

He is loving and leads us in his LOVING-KINDNESS.

I just want you to take a few minutes to adore our Heavenly Father. Open your mouth and tell Him how wonderful He is. Praise Him for who He is and thank Him for at least five things that He has done in your life and your family's lives.

I invite you to pray this prayer today:

Dear Heavenly Father,
Thank You for Your unending love for us. Thank You for Your generosity and for wanting to give us good gifts. Thank You for being a good Father. (Praise Him for some other things about His character). Please heal me in any area that I have a wrong understanding of You. Let me see You for who You truly are!
In Jesus' name, Amen.

DAY 11

God Works Things For Our Good

And we know that in all things God works for the good of those who love him, who have been called according to his purpose.

ROMANS 8:28

When I was twenty-three and had my first child, I had great difficulty breastfeeding. I had a low milk supply and three different breast infections consecutively. I remember literally crying to my husband saying, "Why is this happening to me? Why is this so painful?" And I remember him saying, "I don't know why, but maybe God will use your difficulty to help others one day." I really didn't appreciate his answer that day when I was in pain, but as usual, my husband was so right!

One time I was talking to a new mom who had an emergency c-section. She was feeling guilty and discouraged because she didn't have enough breast milk for her daughter. Once, when she was feeding her daughter a bottle of formula at church, an older mother told her how terrible formula was for her baby. Imagine how awful that made my friend feel, who had had every intention of having a natural birth and exclusively breastfeeding her daughter. I shared my story with her and encouraged her to let go of the guilt. She later told me that my story encouraged her heart and released her from the weight of her and other people's expectations. And as it turns out, her daughter is healthy and thriving!

My breastfeeding story has encouraged countless other moms that I have met throughout the years who were discouraged in this area. Although that season of my life was so dreadfully painful at times, I am so grateful that I have been able to encourage new moms when they encounter difficulties as well. I mean, who can relate to someone whose life seems perfect and everything is in always in order? Often overcoming challenges in our lives is the testimony that encourages those around you.

Whatever difficulty or trial you are facing today, I pray that God meets you. And when you overcome, I believe that you will have a testimony that could encourage others.

I invite you to pray this prayer today:

Dear Heavenly Father,
Thank You for taking everything in our lives and working in them for my good, including my trials. Please use me today to bring encouragement to someone who might need to hear my story or an encouraging word. I love You!
In Jesus' name, Amen.

DAY 12

Power of Words

The tongue has the power of life and death,
and those who love it will eat its fruit.

PROVERBS 18:21

Anyone who knows me, knows that I love to talk. I will be the first to admit though, that sometimes I speak too quickly. I certainly have had to apologize many times in my life for words rashly spoken. I am not writing this devotional because I have fully arrived in this area of my life; rather, I am writing to share with you an area of weakness that I daily try to work on with God and those around me.

In my early twenties, I heard a teaching about how our words have the power to impact our lives, way deeper than I ever imagined. For example, if someone says to a child,

"You are stupid."

"You are ugly."

"You are naughty."

That child, no matter how smart, beautiful, or well-behaved, begins to believe that they are stupid, ugly, and naughty. If others in that child's life speak these harsh words to them, this again reinforces this lie in their life. I think this is part of what Proverbs 18:21 is trying to address. Our words can bring a figurative "life" or "death" to ourselves and to others.

How many of us can remember negative words spoken over us and how it has affected us until we have forgiven the person who spoke it? At the same time, how many of us can remember a kind word from a parent, teacher, or someone else important in our life when we were kids? Listening to encouragement can bring life to a person. On the other hand, agreeing with lies goes against the truth of who God made you.

We have the power and choice to speak life over our kids each day. That is the gift God has given us in being parents. Speak life.

"I believe in you."

"God has called you."

"You are smart."

"You are wonderful."

"You can do all things in Christ."

"You are beautiful/handsome!"

Learning more about the power of our words caused me to be more thoughtful about my words as a person in general, but especially as a wife and mother. Recently a younger mom asked me for parenting advice for her strong-willed four-year-old daughter. I gave her some suggestions, but one of the main things I mentioned was to be intentional with her words. When my kids were younger, if they were acting out, instead of saying to them, "You are bad" or "You are naughty," I would try to say to them, "Hey, I know you are a good boy/girl, so why are you acting naughty? Are you trying to be naughty? How do you think your behavior makes others feel?"

By asking my kids these questions, it often made them actually stop and think about their behavior. As a parent, I never want my kids to define themselves by their behavior, a mistake they have made, or by lies from the enemy. I want them each to be confident in who God made them. This is why, when I correct them, I also try to affirm them about how important they are to me and to God.

Speak words of life over yourself and your family. Take the time to pause and correct your children if you hear them speaking harsh, ungodly words over themselves or their siblings. This is a foundational principle that I encourage every parent to establish in their homes. Our words matter.

I invite you to pray this prayer today:

Dear Heavenly Father,
Please forgive me for any harsh or wrong words spoken.
(Apologize to any of your kids if God is convicting you in this matter). I ask that You cleanse my lips and renew my mind with Your truth. Please let me be a mom who speaks words of life to those around me.
In Jesus' name, Amen.

DAY 13

A Family Tradition

Therefore encourage one another and build each other up, just as in fact you are doing.

1 THESSALONIANS 5:11

Encouraging words and blessings can breathe life into a person. Over the years, I have enjoyed the different small groups that we have been a part of. One of our past small groups had a tradition that when it was someone's birthday, we would take time that week to speak blessings and encouraging words over the birthday person as they enter into a new year.

Several years ago, Chris and I decided to make a new family tradition and do a similar activity with our family on all of our birthdays. When we go out to celebrate one of our birthdays, we take a few minutes and each member of our family says something that they appreciate about that person. It is a simple but sweet time to bring life to the birthday person. I want my kids to be the best of friends to one another. I feel this is definitely one way to help develop deeper friendships among them. If you like this idea, I encourage you to use it in your own families. I often feel emotional during this time at each birthday dinner, and I look forward to it every time.

I want to be more intentional about speaking words of life to family, friends, and any other people I come into contact with. I am often thankful for different things about people in my thoughts, but I might not mention it unless it is a special occasion. Why wait for a special occasion to tell someone what you appreciate and love about them? I am going to look for some way to encourage a friend today. Will you join me and brighten someone's day in your life?

I invite you to pray this prayer today:

Dear Heavenly Father,
Thank You for the gift of encouragement. Please show me someone who needs encouragement today. (When God shows you someone to encourage today, please be faithful to send them a quick text or email and brighten their day.)
In Jesus' name, Amen.

DAY 14

Comparison, Jealousy, Envy

You shall not covet your neighbor's house. You shall not covet your neighbor's wife, or his male or female servant, his ox or donkey, or anything that belongs to your neighbor.

EXODUS 20:17

Most people today wouldn't use the word "covet" but I believe this sin still exists in many of our hearts in the form of comparison, jealousy, and envy.

Theodore Roosevelt said, "Comparison is the thief of joy."

I have found this to be so true when it comes to my children. I feel that when we as mothers get caught in the comparison trap, it not only hurts our own mental state, but it hurts our kids as well.

We can compare our kids to their siblings or to other people's children in so many unhelpful ways: who is sleeping through the night first, who is walking first, who is potty-trained first, who is reading first, who is best behaved. Then as they get older, we focus wrongly on academic, musical, or athletic achievements. Having been in ministry for a long time, I have even seen parents comparing their kids' spirituality. The comparison trap is endless. The devil wants us to be stuck in comparison, envy, and jealousy, but God has a much better way.

When my children were little, I confess that I cared too much about their outward behavior and how others would think about them. But as they got older, I realized the sinfulness in my mindset and behavior and I had to repent to God and my kids. Comparing our kids to others makes them feel insecure and can lead them to believe they are not good enough. It also fails to recognize the unique individual God created them to be and could cause strain in your relationship. Who wants to be around someone who is always comparing them to someone else?

If you have given into the comparison trap like I have in the past, I encourage you to ponder this verse today. Give your insecurities to God and take time to apologize to your children if you feel convicted to.

I invite you to pray this prayer today:

Dear Heavenly Father,
Please forgive me for any ways I have been comparing myself, my family, or my kids to other people. Please help me to stop falling into the comparison trap. Today I choose to surrender myself, my family, and my kids into Your hands. I choose to care about the things You care about. Please show me daily how to raise my kids to love You and to not do things for the opinions of others. In Jesus' name, Amen.

DAY 15

Supernatural Peace

Do not be anxious about anything, but in every situation, by prayer and petition, with thanksgiving, present your requests to God. And the peace of God, which transcends all understanding, will guard your hearts and your minds in Christ Jesus.

PHILIPPIANS 4:6-7

Do you feel overwhelmed with the worries of life? Are concerns about finances keeping you in fear? Are conflicts in marriage making you depressed?

This is a promise God gives to us when we obey Him. This is one of the markers that distinguishes the people of God from the people of this world. There are inevitable storms in life, but during those tumultuous seasons, we can ask God for supernatural strength and peace.

A couple of years ago, my sister Grace was diagnosed with cancer. I was shocked and devastated after hearing this. My sister helped raise me and mothered me in many ways since my parents worked a lot when I was a child. She caught me at the bottom of a hill because she didn't want me to get injured when I was roller skating out of control as a kid and sadly broke her finger in the process. When we were older, I followed her to the same university and she kept an eye out for me there as well.

I immediately started fasting asking God to save her life. This fierce determination rose up in me as I was not going to let the devil shorten her life. I did not know how this would unfold, but I was not going to give up persistently asking God to heal her. Any time I thought about her I started bawling, and I cried for many days. I kept praying Philippians 4:7 over her and her family, that the peace of God, which transcends all understanding, would guard their hearts and minds in Christ Jesus. I would declare this over her and her family daily and insert their names into this scripture.

Thankfully it turned out her cancer was treatable. She ended up only needing a surgery and four rounds of chemotherapy to be healed. One night I was in my minivan, I was still fasting and praying this verse again and immediately the peace of God came into my car. I heard Him say, "Eunice, calm down. I will heal her of this cancer after the surgery." Instantaneously, this incredible peace overcame me, my tears stopped, and I knew that God would heal her. I fasted until her surgery was done and God was true in keeping my heart at peace. When you talk to her family today, they have also expressed having great peace through the whole process and I am grateful for God answering my prayers.

God does not want us to live us in worry, stress, and fear. He wants us to have peace in our hearts, even if the circumstances are bleak. Give God your worries and fears today. Surrender your circumstances that are overwhelming you, and as you obey Him, I really do believe that peace will come in the midst of uncertainty.

I invite you to pray this prayer today:

Dear Heavenly Father,
Thank You for Your peace that is promised for those who obey You. God, I surrender (name the situation or person to Him). I trust You. I will obey You and I ask for

Your supernatural peace to come upon me today. In Jesus' name, Amen.

DAY 16

Weakness

But he said to me, "My grace is sufficient for you, for my power is made perfect in weakness." Therefore I will boast all the more gladly about my weaknesses, so that Christ's power may rest on me. That is why, for Christ's sake, I delight in weaknesses, in insults, in hardships, in persecutions, in difficulties. For when I am weak, then I am strong.

2 CORINTHIANS 12:9-10

I think most human beings hate weakness, or is it just me? I used to think I had life pretty under control, until I became a mom. I could get things done on time. I could make dinner and feed myself, even if it was just cereal. I could sleep through the night and make myself look presentable before leaving the house. Then every possible weakness in my life became glaringly obvious.

When my first son was born, I was not prepared for the sleepless nights. I did not have enough breastmilk production to feed him adequately. I didn't know things about jaundice and babies needing to be hospitalized when their numbers got alarmingly high. I could barely take a shower each day, much less have a meal made for dinner!

No longer could I get to places in a timely manner because I had blowout diapers to change as I was about to put the baby in a car seat. I felt so out of control and weak when my babies would have meltdowns and I didn't know how to soothe them. Or when they became toddlers and would have temper tantrums and I would not know what to do.

Motherhood is such a blessing, but there were many weak times that I had when I wondered where the blessing was. In those moments, I would look at my child's precious face and God would give me renewed strength and hope. Becoming a mom exposes all the selfish parts in our lives. Being a loving, present mother requires great sacrifice. But anything worthwhile in this life takes great work and intention.

When you feel too weak for this job of being a mom, run to our good Father! Ask Him for renewed strength when you feel weak. Ask Him to sustain and refresh you. He loves when we give Him our weaknesses because then He is made strong through us! Give Him the glory!

I invite you to pray this prayer today:

Dear Heavenly Father,
Thank You for loving me in my weakness. I surrender all these places that I feel weak to You! (Name the areas that come to mind where you feel weak). Please replace my weakness with Your great strength. I give You all the glory in my life.
In Jesus' name, Amen.

DAY 17

Stewarding Our God-Dreams

Do not give dogs what is sacred; do not throw your pearls to pigs. If you do, they may trample them under their feet, and turn and tear you to pieces.

MATTHEW 7:6

Has God ever placed a dream in your heart that was inspired by Him? Chris and I have had times in our lives when God has spoken a seemingly huge leap of faith that we have to guard closely. People, even well-meaning Christians can have this tendency to tell us to "be realistic" because they don't understand what God might be calling us to.

For example, homeschooling might seem very foreign to some people. If God has placed this in your heart to do and you are worried about messing up your kids' education, instead of speaking this idea to just anyone in your life, guard the "pearls" the Lord has given you and ask Him to show you who you are to share this dream with. He will be faithful in guiding you.

If God is speaking to you about taking a financial leap of faith and pivoting in your career, don't just share this dream with someone who has never taken a visible leap of faith in their entire lives. Talk to a godly person who also has a track record of stepping out in faith.

If you feel God calling your family to go on missions together, get godly counsel from pastors and other leaders, but make sure to also speak with those who have served overseas. Find a family who has done this and has thrived there, and ask for their wisdom and advice.

Moms, I just want to encourage you to be mindful about the influences you are allowing to speak into your life, especially when it comes to any steps of faith the Lord is leading you to take.

I invite you to pray this prayer today:

Dear Heavenly Father,
Please help me to guard the pearls You have given me.
Show me if there are any unhelpful influences in my life
that You want me to remove. I also pray that You show me
what will keep an atmosphere of faith in our home.
In Jesus' name, Amen.

DAY 18

One Step At A Time

Let love and faithfulness never leave you; bind them around your neck, write them on the tablet of your heart. Then you will win favor and a good name in the sight of God and man. Trust in the Lord with all your heart and lean not on your own understanding; in all your ways submit to him, and he will make your paths straight.

PROVERBS 3:3-6

Knowing that God has a good plan for your life and that His ways are higher than our ways is important for every Christian to understand. This does not mean we will always understand why God leads us in a particular direction, or what the end result will be. But we can have confidence that if we trust in and submit to Him, He will make our paths straight.

When I was twenty-one years old, I heard this minister whom I highly regard speak. She said her biggest life regret was not homeschooling her kids (they were grown at that point) because they could have traveled a lot with her when she ministered around the world instead of being stuck in school.

When I became a mom, her words stuck with me even though Chris and I hadn't started doing much traveling yet. Chris and I decided it would be a good idea if I homeschooled the kids for many reasons, but mainly for the flexibility it offered our family. We moved to Kansas City into a not so desirable neighborhood and I was thankful that I homeschooled because the local schools were not ideal.

Then the Lord called us to the Middle East and I really was in awe of the Lord's kindness in leading us to homeschool. Our transition there was pretty seamless because the kids had the same teacher and the same classmates. I was so grateful that we had already established our homeschool rhythms so that we could make such a massive move without dramatic changes to our children's schooling. When I started my homeschool journey with the kids, I had no clue what travels were ahead for us. I just knew that the Lord wanted us to have flexibility like that minister was talking about. In the early years, I thought that flexibility meant it would be cool to take a trip from New Jersey (where we lived at the time) to Washington D.C. on occasion. I had no clue that the Middle East would be on our horizon ten years later.

When we trust and submit our plans to God, He is so faithful in guiding our steps. What doesn't make sense in one season, will start to make sense in the next season. When we take steps of obedience, His faithful Hand will direct us.

I invite you to pray this prayer today:

Dear Heavenly Father,
I submit my plans to You. I trust You. Please let me hear
Your voice speaking to me and direct and guide my steps.
In Jesus' name, Amen.

DAY 19

Overcoming Fear

Have I not commanded you? Be strong and courageous.
Do not be afraid; do not be discouraged, for the Lord
your God will be with you wherever you go.

JOSHUA 1:9

Several years ago, I bought framed wall art with this scripture to hang in our family loft. I want my kids to always remember that whatever God calls them to, He will be with them. In my younger years as a mom, I was too bound in fear and was overprotective about everything concerning child-rearing. Will formula harm my babies? (I have a medical condition that caused me to not produce enough breast milk for my babies and the guilt tormented me for months when I had my first son). Is sugar, white flour, or white rice terrible for my kids' health? I used to ferment kefir, sprout and grind my own wheat, and bake my own bread. I did lots of random things for what I thought would ensure optimal health. But a lot of this was actually fear-driven and not coming from a healthy place.

Then the Lord delivered me of all of those types of fears when we moved to the Middle East. He made me face them head on. We only lived in the Middle East for three and a half years. When we were leaving, I asked the Lord why He was bringing us back to the U.S. after such a short amount of time. It didn't feel like our presence in that nation made much of an impact. And He told me that our time there was not just for Chris and I to obey His calling; it was for our kids to see the Hand of God moving in their own lives. They saw God deliver our whole family and team through some tumultuous times in that nation. We believe our season overseas was in large part for our kids' hearts, so that when He calls them to do something in faith as they grow older, they will obey Him without hesitation, and 99.9% of the fears that I had, they will not even struggle with.

Are there any fears that are hindering you from stepping out in faith? If so, I encourage you to surrender them to God today. Let today be a marking moment in your life where you hand those fears to God.

I invite you to pray this prayer today:

Dear Heavenly Father,
Please forgive me for living in fear instead of trusting You. I surrender (name the areas you want to surrender over to God). I choose faith over my fears.
In Jesus' name, Amen.

DAY 20

Building Friendships

Two are better than one, because they have a good return for their labor: If either of them falls down, one can help the other up. But pity anyone who falls and has no one to help them up. Also, if two lie down together, they will keep warm. But how can one keep warm alone? Though one may be overpowered, two can defend themselves. A cord of three strands is not quickly broken.

ECCLESIASTES 4:9-12

Friendship is vital to a healthy life. I am so thankful for all of the relationships that God has given me throughout the different seasons of my life. It takes effort to cultivate good friendships, but the reward is immeasurable. It takes sacrifice and sometimes that sacrifice means to go beyond yourself and initiate.

When we first moved away from the East Coast, I was so lonely. It was the first time in my life that I had moved far away from my family and friends. After months of not really making any friends, I decided to initiate a play date with two other moms. We agreed to meet at a nearby playground. As soon as we got situated, one of the moms remarked, "Wow, I am so glad we did this. This is the first play date I have had in a year since moving here!" I was shocked! Almost immediately after this statement, I heard my son screaming. I ran over and he was on the ground crying in pain. He showed me his arm and one of the bones in his forearm was snapped in half from falling off the jungle gym. I was horrified! Well, that was the end of that play date.

The next thing you know, one of the moms was driving us to the hospital because I was holding my son in the back seat and the other mom was leading us to the hospital in her car because I was new to the area and had no idea where to go! That day my son broke his arm was awful, but as I was reflecting on that day, I strongly felt like it was no coincidence that he broke his arm almost immediately after my friend remarked about that being her first play date in a year. In a strange way, all of us frantically taking my son to the emergency room became a real bonding moment. Later, I initiated more play dates with these women and all three of us became very good friends!

I strongly believe that Satan wants us isolated in our own worlds because it is easier for him to attack us. It is inconvenient and intimidating sometimes being the first to initiate a friendship, but if we never overcome our fear or make time, how will we ever cultivate deeper friendships?

About six months after this incident, I decided to invite two moms from our homeschool co-op and their kids over for lunch. The moms had a wonderful time together and the kids had a lot of fun. Later that evening, I noticed my daughter seemed sluggish and feverish. That night, she began vomiting and I knew the flu had arrived. The flu passed through all seven members of our family and about four weeks later, it was finally gone! Once again I was reminded of the importance of praying for protection before play dates, but I also remembered how much the enemy wants to keep us isolated. Satan hates it when we have good friendships because it is that much easier for him to tear us down when we are alone.

I strongly encourage anyone who is lonely to take a step of faith and call someone (an old friend or make a new one). Take the plunge and ask someone out for coffee or make a meal and invite someone to come eat with you! If you are a mom, be the first to initiate a play date at your home or at a park! If the first person you ask says no, don't waste time being hurt or offended, just ask someone else. I really believe you and someone else will be blessed by your efforts!

I invite you to pray this prayer today:

Dear Heavenly Father,
I pray that You would open a door for a new friendship today.
I choose to step out in faith and bless someone else today.
In Jesus' name, Amen.

DAY 21

Memorial Stones

So Joshua called together the twelve men he had appointed from the Israelites, one from each tribe, and said to them, "Go over before the ark of the Lord your God into the middle of the Jordan. Each of you is to take up a stone on his shoulder, according to the number of the tribes of the Israelites, to serve as a sign among you. In the future, when your children ask you, 'What do these stones mean?' tell them that the flow of the Jordan was cut off before the ark of the covenant of the Lord. When it crossed the Jordan, the waters of the Jordan were cut off. These stones are to be a memorial to the people of Israel forever."

JOSHUA 4:4-7

Do you have a good memory? I feel like it's a common joke among moms that as we have kids, lose sleep, and are tired often, that our memory goes out the window! As I have gotten older and am now in my mid-forties, I believe this is just an issue with all human beings. I think that is why the Lord asked Joshua and the Israelites to establish these memory stones.

Have you ever prayed for something to happen, God answers

your prayer, but then you completely forget that it happened? And then you just move on with your next prayer request? And then you get discouraged because you feel like God doesn't listen to you or answer your prayers? I know I have done this time and time again.

That's why it's important to write things down. I am terrible at journaling. I have so many partially-used journals. As a New Year's resolution I decide, "I'm gonna journal everything this new year" and then by February my journal is forgotten and collecting dust. Am I the only one? If journaling is too hard for you to be consistent with, write notes in your phone. Write notes in your phone of when God answers your prayers.

Even as I am writing this, the Lord is reminding me of an answered prayer that I didn't write down, and it's making me cry thinking about it. One year, we had a rough Christmas season. A lot of incredibly hard transitions were happening in our life. Our Christmases are simple as we have five kids, but it is a high priority for me to make sure my kids receive some small things that they want for Christmas. That year as Christmas was approaching, an acquaintance reached out to my husband. He is a fellow minister and he said he knew Christmas gifts could be lean some years for minister's kids and that he and his wife wanted to bless our children. He gave $100 per kid to each of our five children that year, just for fun. When our kids opened up all their gifts and then we handed them this last one to open, it was so heartwarming to see their faces light up in surprise. This generous gift from our acquaintances meant a lot to me because it felt like the Lord just kissed us and said, "Hey, I see your family. I know this is a hard time, but you are not forgotten."

I invite you to pray this prayer today:

Dear Heavenly Father,
I'm sorry for all the times I have forgotten when You have answered my prayers and provided for me. I pray that today You would help me recall these testimonies.

In Jesus' name, Amen.

(As the Lord helps you to remember these testimonies, I encourage you to write them down in your phone or in a journal and read it whenever you need some inspiration!)

DAY 22

Wonderfully Made

For you created my inmost being; you knit me together in my mother's womb. I praise you because I am fearfully and wonderfully made; your works are wonderful, I know that full well. My frame was not hidden from you when I was made in the secret place, when I was woven together in the depths of the earth.

PSALM 139:13-15

Do you believe this scripture? Do you believe that God's works are wonderful and that includes YOU?

When our babies are born and come into our home (biological or adopted), we as mothers instinctively look at them and think they are the cutest things in the world. Every good mother that I know thinks this way. It is just a natural overflow of our overwhelming love for them. When we read this scripture and look into the beautiful eyes of our children, we think, "Oh of course, God Your works are wonderful, look how wonderfully adorable this child is!"

But today I want you take this scripture and apply it to yourself. This scripture says that God's works are wonderful. Can you believe that He made you wonderfully? I find a lot of us moms naturally think these types of thoughts about our kids, but we cannot connect to them on a heart level for ourselves.

Today I challenge you to take a few minutes and ask God to help you understand and believe you are made "fearfully" and "wonderfully." God made your height, your body size, your ethnicity, your eye color, and your hair color. He delights in you. Do you delight in who He created you to be? If there are any false beliefs and lies about yourself that you are recognizing today, I want you to give them to God.

I think this is so important for moms to understand because all healthy moms want our kids to understand these things about themselves. "God made you fearfully! God made you wonderfully!" As we try to impart this truth to our kids, I really believe they will never be able to fully grasp this if we as moms stay insecure about who God created us to be.

I invite you to pray this prayer today:

***Dear Heavenly Father,
I repent for believing false beliefs and lies about myself (list any false beliefs and lies that come to your mind right now and give them to God). Please help me to see Your truth about me today.
In Jesus' name, Amen.***

DAY 23

Shining Like Gold

So Shadrach, Meshach and Abednego came out of the fire, and the satraps, prefects, governors and royal advisers crowded around them. They saw that the fire had not harmed their bodies, nor was a hair of their heads singed; their robes were not scorched, and there was no smell of fire on them. Then Nebuchadnezzar said, "Praise be to the God of Shadrach, Meshach and Abednego, who has sent his angel and rescued his servants! They trusted in him and defied the king's command and were willing to give up their lives rather than serve or worship any god except their own God."

DANIEL 3:26B-28

One time the Lord spoke to me through this story and said, "Eunice, learn from those who have gone through the fire and have come out shining like gold."

Why didn't God save Shadrach, Meshach, and Abednego *before* they got thrown into the fire? God could have halted this scenario at any given point but He chose to save them *after* they endured the furnace. Why did these events have to unfold in this incredibly intense manner?

One concept that is sometimes hard for me to accept about

life is that trials and testing inevitably come. The Bible is very clear about this, but it's still challenging for me to accept because I don't like pain. Who does? But as I have grown in the Lord, I know that consistently in scripture, it says that trials are unavoidable.

One time when we were going through some challenging trials in life, listening to other people's testimonies really helped encourage me. Unexpected and very real loneliness, heartbreak through broken relationships, and dramatic financial loss, all came crashing at our doorstep at once. These were all very unwelcome and challenging circumstances, but listening to stories of how others endured their fiery challenges would uplift my heart. I would read and listen to testimonies of how God came through for others and be strengthened to keep enduring and keep moving forward.

If you are going through a fiery test right now, I encourage you to do the same. Don't listen to the critical, pessimistic voices in your life. Block them out if you have to for a season. Listen to those voices that will bring you life and hope. God will faithfully help you endure this trial. Lean on Him and be encouraged by those who have gone before you and are shining like gold after their trial.

I invite you to pray this prayer today:

Dear Heavenly Father,
I trust You in this trial. I trust that if I keep leaning on You that You will help me endure this pain. I will come out of this hardship shining like gold and will have a testimony that will encourage others in the future. I love You Lord!
In Jesus' name, Amen.

DAY 24

Give It To God

Humble yourselves, therefore, under God's mighty hand, that he may lift you up in due time. Cast all your anxiety on him because he cares for you.

1 PETER 5:6-7

In one of our last weeks in the Middle East, Chris got pickpocketed and his wallet stolen on the crowded subway. It was violating and also so frustrating because he lost his driver's license, his visa that he was supposed to carry everywhere as a foreigner, and about one hundred dollars in cash. This unexpected event also caused us to miss the last ferry ride back home. We had no choice but to hail a taxi, which would cost a lot more than the ferry would have. There was a lot of traffic driving home in the taxi, but what ended an already bad night was that we got completely scammed by the taxi driver and he stole extra money from us.

I was so stressed and anxious and although I kept trying to give this injustice to the Lord, I spent a few days in depression. Humbling ourselves before the Lord sometimes involves trusting Him to bring justice to a situation, rather than seeking vengeance ourselves. It is a proactive surrender. Once I cast all of my anxiety upon Him, I was able to have a measure of peace again.

A few days after this incident, a kind friend gave us an envelope with the sweetest note. Inside the card was a cash gift in U.S. Dollars to our family. When I exchanged the money to the local currency, it was almost exactly the amount that was stolen from us that night. This felt like a gift directly from God's hand saying, "Eunice, I got you guys. You can trust me even when you are sinned against."

God is so kind in giving us these sweet kisses, exactly when we need them. Moms, let us humble ourselves and entrust Him with all the worries and cares that steal our peace. If we do this, God promises to meet us in His due time.

I invite you to pray this prayer today:

***Dear Heavenly Father,
I choose to humble myself before You today. Please forgive me for not humbling myself in the past. God I entrust You with (speak out all your worries and cares to Him right now) and I leave them here at Your feet. I trust You and I love You! Thank You for being trustworthy.
In Jesus' name, Amen.***

DAY 25

Thankfulness

And whatever you do, whether in word or deed,
do it all in the name of the Lord Jesus, giving
thanks to God the Father through him.

COLOSSIANS 3:17

Sometimes we need an attitude adjustment, both moms and children! On any given day, moms and kids can get cranky, irritable, and easily angered. God gave me this idea once as the kids got older and their writing ability improved. On cranky days, I made my kids grab a notebook and write "thankfulness lists." They had to write down ten things they were grateful for and this helped them make an attitude adjustment.

I want to help each of my kids grow as an overall person and mature in the Lord. If any of my kids that are over the age of five need an attitude adjustment because they are exhibiting signs of ungratefulness or crankiness that leads to fights with their siblings, I have them do thankfulness lists. I think that these lists help tremendously. It forces them to take a time out, regain their self-control, and reflect about how their life really isn't all that horrible. If your kids aren't old enough to write well yet, you can also have them draw pictures for their thankfulness list.

As an adult, thankfulness is something that is imperative to cultivate. Ungratefulness and ungodly discontentment are sins that can plague any of us. Thankfulness is something that God highly values and as a mom, I want to help instill this in our children. Thankfulness helps all of us realign our hearts to see the many blessings that God has given us.

I encourage you to take five minutes today and write down in your phone or journal ten things that you are grateful for today. This activity helps me when I feel stressed and weary and I think it will refresh you as well.

I invite you to pray this prayer today:

Dear Heavenly Father,
Please forgive me for any ungratefulness in my heart. I choose to be thankful for the blessings in my life today. (Thank Him for those ten things right now). Please realign my heart to be grateful. In Jesus' name, Amen.

DAY 26

Waiting On God

But do not forget this one thing, dear friends: With the Lord a day is like a thousand years, and a thousand years are like a day. The Lord is not slow in keeping his promise, as some understand slowness. Instead he is patient with you, not wanting anyone to perish, but everyone to come to repentance.

2 PETER 3:8-9

Is there a promise God has given you but you are still waiting for it to be fulfilled? Something concerning your marriage? A promise over your finances? A prophetic word about your children? Or anything else concerning your future?

I love how this scripture tells us that God is not slow in keeping his promises. While this verse specifically refers to the return of Jesus, I believe it reveals in a general sense something of the character and ways of God. His thoughts are truly not our thoughts. And as frustrating it is at times, the truth is that His timetable is not our timetable.

One time I prayed for this young woman. She told me that she was confused about the promises that God spoke to her in her life. She shared all about the different things He had said. I could sense her frustration and weariness, so I offered to pray for her. As I began to pray for her, the Lord immediately spoke to me in His quiet voice, "Eunice, she is not confused; she is just tired of waiting." I immediately felt to just pray for patience while waiting on God.

As someone who loves to just get things done, I struggle with patience. But I have learned over and over again that the Lord's timing is indeed not our timing. I just want to encourage any mom who is in a waiting season: do not give up. Cling to the promises of God in your life. Look through the scriptures and find some verses to cling onto in the waiting! Put your hand to the plow with whatever is before you and do not give up. His leadership and timing are perfect.

I invite you to pray this prayer today:

Dear Heavenly Father,
Give me patience and grace for the waiting. I trust You and I trust that Your timing is perfect. Help me to cling to You whenever I want to give up and give me strength to keep moving forward when I am waiting on You.
In Jesus' name, Amen.

DAY 27

Kingdom Generosity

One person gives freely, yet gains even more; another withholds unduly, but comes to poverty. A generous person will prosper; whoever refreshes others will be refreshed.

PROVERBS 11:24-25

Generosity is such an important Kingdom principle. God is a good Father who loves to give, and in His incredible generosity, He sent His Son Jesus to save us. Generosity is part of His nature, and we as the people of God are called to be like Him in this way.

Motherhood is one of the greatest areas where we can learn to be generous and sacrificial. We pour ourselves out day in and day out. When babies are young, we even pour ourselves out in the night watches. It is a beautiful thing for us to give to our families generously. When we give freely to our families, God takes note of every sacrifice that we make. He sees every diaper we change. He sees each meal that we prepare. He sees when we help our kids with their homework. He sees it all!

I believe that it is so important to be generous to our family and to others. As we pour into our kids, I think it is crucial for us to teach our kids to be generous as well. This can happen in so many different ways: in giving financial offerings (above our tithe) and encouraging our children to do so as well; in helping others and including our kids in those actions; inviting people over for dinner and having our children help us set up and cook; in finding practical ways to serve a family in need.

One time I cooked for a new neighbor whose husband was away for military service and she was quite sick. Any time a mom gets sick, it is hard on the family, but flying solo while you are under the weather is a whole other level. I am so deeply grateful to our military families for their sacrifice and service. When I heard she was sick, I randomly cooked a simple meal and dropped it off at their doorstep. I didn't think much about it afterwards. But several months later, my son babysat for their family and she told him how thankful she was towards our family for the time we cooked for them. I really had no immediate recollection of cooking for her, but then I was reminded of that very simple gesture. It meant so much to her and she paid my son very handsomely for his babysitting. My son came home that night thanking me for being an example to him about being generous to others, not just because he got paid well, but because he realized how even small things can be very meaningful to others.

I share this story not to brag about my life. I share this testimony because God wants us to be generous. He is generous with us and this is one way we show His love to the world around us. Let's teach our kids through example and guide them to see this attribute of God.

I invite you to pray this prayer today:

Dear Heavenly Father,
Please teach me ways to be generous to my own family and to the world around me. Please help me be obedient to Your promptings when You invite me to be generous.

In Jesus' name, Amen.

DAY 28

Light Of The World

You are the light of the world. A town built on a hill cannot be hidden. Neither do people light a lamp and put it under a bowl. Instead they put it on its stand, and it gives light to everyone in the house. In the same way, let your light shine before others, that they may see your good deeds and glorify your Father in heaven.

MATTHEW 5:14-16

When you watch the news, do you feel overwhelmed by the darkness and sadness in this world? This world is so broken and we need all need more of Jesus. Moms, we have such an important role in this world. We need the light of godly, Christian homes to shine brightly as a testimony to this dark world. This is a vision for every Jesus-loving family to keep before them.

Raising my kids to love Jesus, have confidence in who God uniquely made them to be, and love others around them is no small feat. When we as parents pour the love and instruction of the Bible into our children, they will thrive and grow in any sphere God plants them in. We are raising up the next generation of Daniels, Josephs, Calebs, Esthers, Deborahs, and Ruths in our own homes. That is an amazing responsibility and privilege.

A few years ago, I attended parent teacher conferences for my three teenage sons. This was one of the best days of my life; it felt like Christmas! I loved hearing about how my kids are doing in school, not just academically, but how they are growing in character, responsibility, and kindness in ways that I never get to see. But the teachers shared things with me that they saw and noticed in each of my sons. It was a day that I got to hear about the good fruit of their lives, the result of the seeds in them day in and day out when they were little. Now the sweet fruit is apparent and bringing refreshment to others.

This beautiful day made me cry driving home at the faithfulness of the Lord to our family. As a mom, when your kids are little and you are nurturing them each monotonous day, you are left to wonder if making food, changing diapers, cleaning their constant messes, teaching them to pick up their toys, correcting them, or breaking up fights with their siblings, makes any difference in their lives or to the world. The mundane things that seemed so meaningless at times were indeed bearing real fruit.

I often have young couples ask me how we decided to have five kids. Is this number something we planned or did it just happen? We planned to have five kids. Yes, we were tired, exhausted, and stretched financially. But God put a long-term vision in me and Chris, that we would be blessed having these five children and that we indeed will impact the world around us through our kids.

I do not know yet what each of my children will become when they are independent adults, but they are all growing into fine young people. I have faith that as Chris and I keep sowing into their precious lives, that one day they will change the world because they will be bringing His light into each and every space they are called to.

I just want to encourage every mother reading this, don't lose heart! You are making a profound difference in the lives of your beautiful children. I pray that the Lord strengthens and encourages you today!

I invite you to pray this prayer today:

Dear Heavenly Father,
Thank You for the blessing of each of my children. Thank You for seeing every small seed that I have planted into my children's lives. I pray that it will bear good fruit. Help me gain a vision for how You want to use my kids to change this world. Thank You that even though this world is dark, You will use my children and our family to shine your light in the dark places. Please teach me how to partner with You in raising these world changers for Your glory.
In Jesus' name, Amen.

DAY 29

Healing Prayer

Is anyone among you in trouble? Let them pray. Is anyone happy? Let them sing songs of praise. Is anyone among you sick? Let them call the elders of the church to pray over them and anoint them with oil in the name of the Lord. And the prayer offered in faith will make the sick person well; the Lord will raise them up. If they have sinned, they will be forgiven. Therefore confess your sins to each other and pray for each other so that you may be healed. The prayer of a righteous person is powerful and effective.

JAMES 5:13-16

The Bible teaches us that there is power in prayer. There is healing in prayer. There is healing in praying in community together, with others. I believe in getting in a solid church community to grow together. This is something so important for parents, and for our children as well.

I remember when I was going through a rough time rebuilding trust in relationships. I had gone through a painful and challenging time in some friendships in my life. We were intentionally flying under the radar at our huge church. Each week you could find us sitting in the back, leaving as soon as the sermon ended so that we wouldn't interact with anyone.

One night I had a dream that I was meeting with our pastor and I was telling her about the painful period we had been through. When I woke up from the dream, I knew I should meet up with her even though I was very hesitant because I had fear of trusting someone I didn't know well. Thankfully she made time for me in her busy schedule to meet at a coffee shop. When we met up, I just jumped in and shared what I was sharing with her in the dream as I did not want to waste an invitation from the Lord to be healed. She lovingly encouraged me and prayed for me.

Something definitely shifted in my heart that day. I felt a new courage to be vulnerable to people again. I felt healing in my heart from her empathic response and as she vulnerably shared parts of her story that I could identify with. There is power in praying alone before God. But there is also power and healing that comes when we confess our sins and pain to another person.

Mommas, we are not meant to do life alone. If you feel stuck in your spiritual life, or if you just need some prayer, reach out to another trustworthy mom, friend, or spiritual leader and ask for prayer. God desires to bring true healing and restoration in our lives.

I invite you to pray this prayer today:

Dear Heavenly Father,
Please open my heart to godly community and accountability. Thank You that You give us friendships to deepen our growth and bring healing to our lives. Please open my eyes to a trustworthy community around me and let me be faithful in reaching out to others and for myself when I need it. I love You Lord!
In Jesus' name, Amen.

DAY 30

Burdens

Come to me, all you who are weary and burdened, and I will give you rest. Take my yoke upon you and learn from me, for I am gentle and humble in heart, and you will find rest for your souls. For my yoke is easy and my burden is light.

MATTHEW 11:28-30

Do you feel weary and burdened? Being a mom has so many challenges, and it can be physically and mentally exhausting. Rest is not something that comes easily to moms, is it? But Jesus promises to give us rest if we bring Him our burdens. I am so grateful for His unending kindness to us.

We serve and pour out every day. We cook multiple times per day to feed ourselves and our families. We repeatedly clean all the crumbs that are spread around the house. We do seemingly endless loads of laundry. We shuttle our kids to school, to homeschool coops, to lessons, to sports, and many other things!

Jesus says that His yoke is *easy* and His burden is *light*! If you are overwhelmed by the craziness of your life, I encourage you to pull back and spend time with Him, while doing your dishes, laundry, cooking, or driving. Give Him everything that is burdening you. He doesn't want you to live in endless survival mode; He wants to give you rest.

Notice that when we give our burdens to Him, He is not harshly telling us to "do better," "do more," or "what you have done is not enough."

Yet some of us have that harsh voice in our head, criticizing us for not doing better and not doing more. Whose voice is this?

As moms we need to be discerning about whose voice we are listening to. If we choose to listen to the enemy, then that will trickle into our lives and parenting. But if we choose the voice of Jesus, He will bring light into our lives and parenting. Choose whose voice you will listen to today.

If you spend time with Him, maybe He will speak to you about some unnecessary things that He wants you to eliminate out of your life. Things that are clogging your attention and sucking energy from your schedule. Maybe He will convict you of certain sins. Or maybe He is saying, just lay your worries down. I have a sinful tendency to be a worry wart instead of giving my concerns to Him. I have sadly wasted many hours stewing in fear, doubt, and worry about our future. God doesn't want us to live this way! These things add unnecessary burdens to our lives.

Take time to pause today and give your worries and cares to Him.

I invite you to pray this prayer today:

Dear Heavenly Father,
Please forgive me for carrying my burdens on my own.
I trust You. Today I give all of my worries and burdens
to You. (List them all now and surrender them to Him).
Today I choose Your rest and I receive Your yoke.
In Jesus' name, Amen.

DAY 31

God Can Equip Us

Moses said to the Lord, "Pardon your servant, Lord. I have never been eloquent, neither in the past nor since you have spoken to your servant. I am slow of speech and tongue." The Lord said to him, "Who gave human beings their mouths? Who makes them deaf or mute? Who gives them sight or makes them blind? Is it not I, the Lord? Now go; I will help you speak and will teach you what to say."

EXODUS 4:10-12

Have you ever felt inadequate? Regardless of how confident you felt as a person before becoming a mom, I think almost every mom would agree that when they became a mom of one, two, three, or more, at some point you felt inadequate. Not enough. Limited. Selfish. Broken. Unable to accomplish the daily tasks ahead of you.

Moses is listed as a hero in the faith in Hebrews 11, but these were his humble beginnings. He felt inadequate for the task that God was calling him to, but God is the one who carried Him through. God promised He would be with Him.

The Bible tells us that God is the same yesterday, today, and forever. Moms, if God equipped Moses for the assignment that was ahead of him, He most certainly can and will equip you. Motherhood is a daunting assignment and a high call. We are entrusted with the lives of these incredible tiny humans and most of us don't know what we are doing!

Ask God for Him to fill you with His grace. Lean into his voice to daily guide you in raising your children. Commit each of your children unto the Lord. God picked you to be your child's mom and He will faithfully equip you for each day ahead if you ask Him!

I invite you to pray this prayer today:

Dear Heavenly Father,
Please equip me each day for the assignment You have given me to be a godly mother to my children. I commit (name each of your kids here) into Your Hands. Show me how to raise them to love You and to walk in Your ways.
In Jesus' name, Amen.

DAY 32

Teach Our Kids To Pray

He said to them, "Go into all the world and preach the gospel to all creation. Whoever believes and is baptized will be saved, but whoever does not believe will be condemned. And these signs will accompany those who believe: In my name they will drive out demons; they will speak in new tongues; they will pick up snakes with their hands; and when they drink deadly poison, it will not hurt them at all; they will place their hands on sick people, and they will get well."

MARK 16:15-18

I am so grateful that God loves every single one of us, no matter our age! He listens to our prayers! I believe a crucial part of raising our children is to teach them to read the Bible and to pray. Personal prayer is vital but also praying for others is so important.

One time after our fourth child was born, Chris lifted her stroller to walk up the stairs at church and hurt his back. He twisted it awkwardly and was in tremendous pain for about a week. Finally, he couldn't take the pain any longer, and he asked our three older boys to pray for him. They were about five, four, and three years old at the time. We asked them each to take turns laying hands on his back and praying. The boys listened to us and prayed for Chris' back to be healed. I don't think any of us expected anything to happen, but much to all of our surprise, God healed Chris' hurting back in that exact moment! God answered the prayers of our precious sons; it was a miracle!

When we teach our kids from a young age the importance of prayer and how to pray from a young age, it will become a natural part of who they are. Teach and lead them from your example. When something happens of concern, gather the children and pray together. When someone is sick, have each kid pray for them. When it is meal time, pray together and thank God for the food.

I am eternally grateful to my parents for teaching me the importance of reading the Bible and praying regularly when I was a kid. I saw them faithfully doing these things every day my entire life. I also witnessed them living for God as best as they could every day of my life. Their witness and these spiritual disciplines were essential in helping me to decide to follow Jesus as a teen. I am thankful that Chris and I have imparted this to our children and I pray that in the future, they will pass this legacy to our grandchildren.

I invite you to pray this prayer today:

Dear Heavenly Father,
Thank You that You are a God who heals, saves, and delivers.
Please give me courage to step out in faith and pray for
others, and to teach my children to do the same.
In Jesus' name, Amen.

DAY 33

Christ Our Foundation

By wisdom a house is built, and through understanding it is established; through knowledge its rooms are filled with rare and beautiful treasures.

PROVERBS 24:3-4

One day I was walking through a home décor store and saw this scripture framed. I started tearing up because I felt the Lord speaking to me. There are so many things in this world vying for our attention. There are numerous value systems and theories that we can establish our homes upon. God's divine love, wisdom, and understanding is what we as parents should build our house upon, because how else will our homes withstand the ups and downs that inevitably come in life?

Job transitions, housing moves, school changes, financial losses and gains, sickness, marriage conflicts, learning disabilities, sleep problems in our kids, dietary allergies – there are so many things that can happen in life. If we don't build on the foundation of Jesus in our households, our homes will inevitably collapse.

When we build our homes on the foundation of Christ, we are wise builders (Matthew 7:24-27). And when we teach our children about the character and ways of God, it lays a foundation for their future where they will hopefully continue to walk with God and trust in Him.

Moms, I cannot encourage you enough to keep laying a good foundation in your children. At the end of our lives, we will never regret the time we spent nurturing our kids, teaching them about God, and being the primary influence in their lives.

What we invest into our kids each day has the potential to last not just here on earth, but for eternity. Isn't that amazing and scary all at the same time? When my kids were little, life was really challenging. I was tired, cranky, and exhausted. One day I remember having a particularly rough day. My second son was around two years old and was barely making sentences, but out of nowhere, he grabbed my leg and said very articulately, "MOM! I NEED YOU!" It shocked me at first, but I felt like the Lord was speaking to me through him to re-align my cranky heart.

The monotony of motherhood was wearing me down. We pour and pour into our kids and see minimal effect in the day to day. Sometimes it takes many years to see if what we are doing has any impact. But I encourage every mom reading this that what we are doing absolutely matters. Have faith that the foundation we are laying will endure.

I invite you to pray this prayer today:

Dear Heavenly Father,
Thank You for these beautiful treasures that You have entrusted me with in this life. Please teach me how to build a godly foundation in the lives of my children and in my home.
In Jesus' name, Amen.

DAY 34

Nothing Can Stop His Love

Who shall separate us from the love of Christ? Shall trouble or hardship or persecution or famine or nakedness or danger or sword? As it is written: "For your sake we face death all day long; we are considered as sheep to be slaughtered." No, in all these things we are more than conquerors through him who loved us. For I am convinced that neither death nor life, neither angels nor demons, neither the present nor the future, nor any powers, neither height nor depth, nor anything else in all creation, will be able to separate us from the love of God that is in Christ Jesus our Lord.

ROMANS 8:35-39

Isn't it amazing that nothing, nothing at all can separate us from God's love? That is an incredible promise to stand upon, especially when we feel unlovable. The promise brings hope when we need hope and feel like a failure. The truth is, none of us are perfect moms, so I am so grateful for God's love and grace that sustain us.

When we get angry with our kids, God's love is still the same. He is so willing to offer us His forgiveness when we repent.

When we lose our peace and start going down the bunny trail

of worry, His love is still there for us.

God knows we are going to fail, but He loves us anyway. Isn't that incredible?

Have you ever felt like you have failed? Failed God? Your kids? Others in your life? Oftentimes when this happens, we want to hide away in our shame. We often want to hide from God and others. But I want to encourage you to take time today to ask God to give you a fresh revelation on His love for you. Having His love and acceptance is something that can carry us through the hardest, most difficult days and trials.

Run into His loving arms my friends!

I invite you to pray this prayer today:

Dear Heavenly Father,
Thank You for Your great love. Thank You that nothing can separate me from Your love. Give me a fresh revelation of Your love today.
In Jesus' name, Amen.

DAY 35

Enemies?

But love your enemies, do good to them, and lend to them without expecting to get anything back. Then your reward will be great, and you will be children of the Most High, because he is kind to the ungrateful and wicked. Be merciful, just as your Father is merciful.

LUKE 6:35-36

God talks about forgiving others throughout the Bible. Who are our "enemies"? Sometimes I don't think it is as clear as we might think. An enemy can be someone who has hurt us deeply and never said sorry. It could be a person who is just contentious in our life, or someone who was abusive to us. These are all people that can become "enemies" to us in our hearts.

God says He will reward us if we forgive. It's for our own good. It's one way we show His incredible love to the world around us. There are so many opportunities to forgive in life. You might need to forgive that person that cut you off in the morning commute or school drop off. You might need to forgive a parent who didn't parent you in a godly manner. Maybe you need to forgive that person that you really thought was a friend but betrayed you. Maybe you need to forgive that pastor or mentor or church that wounded you deeply. There are so many opportunities for us to be hurt in this broken world, but moms I encourage you to forgive or your bitterness will overflow to your kids.

There have been times in my life that I have been betrayed and heartbroken over severed relationships. Relationships that I thought were centered around God were broken. God led me to forgive over and over again and release them into the freedom of my forgiveness every time I thought of them. And over time as I did this the sting became less and less and healing came. It did not come overnight, but over months and years of releasing their actions and them up to God, healing came.

Even as you read this, God might be showing you people you have to forgive in your life. It could be something from long ago or more recent. Don't brush past this moment. Take the time to forgive them and be freed in Jesus!

I invite you to pray this prayer today:

Dear Heavenly Father,
Thank You for Your love and forgiveness. I thank You that You are merciful, so with Your power I can be merciful to others as well. Today, I choose to forgive (fill in the blank) for (tell the Lord how you were hurt and list the reasons before Him. He is a wonderful listener!). I forgive this person and I release them fully into the freedom of my forgiveness. Please heal me of my wounds. In Jesus' name, Amen.

(You might have to say this prayer multiple times for days and months, but I do believe that if you forgive and surrender your pain to God, He will heal you!)

DAY 36

Forgetting What Lies Behind

Brothers and sisters, I do not consider myself yet to have taken hold of it. But one thing I do: Forgetting what is behind and straining toward what is ahead, I press on toward the goal to win the prize for which God called me heavenward in Christ Jesus.

PHILIPPIANS 3:13-14

Apostle Paul gives us some incredible advice in these verses. "Forgetting what is behind" is imperative for us if we are to move ahead in our faith and lives. Our pasts, both failures and successes, can hold us back from what God is calling us to in our everyday lives.

For moms, I think a big temptation for us is to think about what our lives used to be like when we were single and without kids. The world was open and we could pick up and do whatever we wanted, whenever we wanted. We used to be able to take a trip when we wanted, give as much to our careers as we wanted, go on dates with our husbands when we wanted, go shopping with our friends or by ourselves, be more involved in serving at church, or even something as simple as taking a shower when we wanted.

A lot changed when we became moms. Now we have these tiny people in our lives who are completely dependent on us for their survival and wellbeing! They rely on us for everything, so our lives look drastically different. Like everything in life, when planning something, the more people involved, more juggling is required.

A massive cause of discontentment that I have experienced personally and have seen in other young moms is comparison. Not just comparing ourselves to other moms which makes us miserable, but comparing our current lives to our former lives. When we had "freedoms" in our past that we no longer have now, and constantly look back on those "good old days," we get stuck.

I think that is why Apostle Paul charges us to forget the former things, good or bad, and strain towards what is ahead!

God has abundant grace for you in this current season you are in! Take hold of that grace! Ask Him for more grace when your tank feels low. He is faithful to meet you exactly where you are. God gave you these beautiful children in His perfect timetable. Don't waste any more time looking back at your former life, give thanks for the blessings in your current life.

I invite you to pray this prayer today:

Dear Heavenly Father,
Please forgive me for comparing myself with others and comparing my current life to my past life. I choose to stop looking back and choose to be thankful for today. Please give me grace to press forward and grow in You.
In Jesus' name, Amen.

DAY 37

Desert Seasons

I will make rivers flow on barren heights, and springs within the valleys. I will turn the desert into pools of water, and the parched ground into springs. I will put in the desert the cedar and the acacia, the myrtle and the olive. I will set junipers in the wasteland, the fir and the cypress together, so that people may see and know, may consider and understand, that the hand of the Lord has done this, that the Holy One of Israel has created it.

ISAIAH 41:18-20

Have you ever been in a "desert" season? Where you have felt lost and dry and you're looking for the Lord to speak, but all you see before you is a vast desert, with no oasis in sight?

I got to go camping in the desert with friends in the Middle East last year. Driving through that desolate place was something like I had never seen. Picture just endless sand and barrenness. No water anywhere. No people around. I felt like I was plopped in the middle of a movie with my friends, so far away from home (later I found out that some movies were actually filmed there). It felt eerie to me and it made all the desert imagery in the Bible come alive with new meaning.

If we keep pressing into God, He promises that the waters of His Spirit will flow, even in the desert.

When I was a young mom, I went through very dry seasons. I couldn't figure out how to thrive in my desert season. Partly, I needed healing from my past. I pursued inner healing counseling and that helped a lot. I was also pretty sleep deprived for many years and I just felt like a zombie. (One thing I can never teach is how to get your kids to sleep through the night before the age of two. I failed at this with all five of my children.) Condemning myself didn't help me draw closer to God. Guilt in my parenting plagued me until I surrendered all of my failures to the Lord.

Something I am glad I didn't do in that season was give up. God loves us and He is so much kinder to us than any of us can imagine. Run into His arms and ask Him to make the rivers and springs flow in your life! Ask Him to grow things in your wasteland! Give praise to Him in the deserts of our lives!

I invite you to pray this prayer today:

Dear Heavenly Father,
Please send Your Holy Spirit rivers and springs into my desert. Please grow things deep in me in this season.
Please give me the grace to never give up!
In Jesus' name, Amen.

DAY 38

Motherly Love

Just as a nursing mother cares for her children, so we cared for you. Because we loved you so much, we were delighted to share with you not only the gospel of God but our lives as well.

1 THESSALONIANS 2:7B-8

I was a latchkey kid with immigrant parents. My parents worked endless hours to provide for our family. I am so grateful for the sacrifices they made to come to the United States to give me and my sisters a better life. But because they worked such long hours at their store, I was a lonely kid. Like most immigrants, my sisters and I were left to take care of ourselves for most of each day. That's where I am thankful for my friends' moms. When I was a kid, I can distinctly think of three different mothers of my good friends who made a huge impact on my life.

God used them to show me His love in very meaningful ways as a child. These moms joyfully welcomed me into their homes after school. They generously fed me whenever I was at their houses. They sacrificially gave me rides each week when I needed them. They were not all stay-at-home moms. They were just involved moms who saw a lonely kid and generously loved me in these practical ways. I am deeply grateful to them even as an adult for their kindness. Their impact on my life is what gave me a vision as a child to nurture my future children in ways that I missed out on.

I believe that generous hospitality is one way that we can share God's love with others around us. Moms, we are created and wired to bring nurture and love to every space that we are called to: our homes, workplaces, communities, neighborhoods, churches, etc. You might be in a season where you only have enough energy to keep up with your own kids, and that's totally fine. But if you have the bandwidth, loving and serving other kids will impact them in ways you could never imagine.

I invite you to pray this prayer today:

Dear Heavenly Father,
Help me to show Your love through generosity and hospitality.
Show me ways that I can be Your hands and feet not only
to my own family, but to those around me as well.
In Jesus' name, Amen.

DAY 39

Encourage One Another

But encourage one another daily, as long as it is called "Today," so that none of you may be hardened by sin's deceitfulness.

HEBREWS 3:13

God created us for relationships. Jesus died so that we could have a restored relationship with the Father and with one another. Through our love others will see God's love. We are not meant to do life alone. If you are living in isolation, it is much easier for the devil to come and devour you. I believe that when we sit by ourselves in our pain and isolation, there are too many ways that our perspectives can get skewed. Lies that should be corrected become truths in our hearts.

Our world really values independence, but the Bible says to "encourage one another daily." Some people might look at encouraging one another daily as unnecessary or weak, but we are encouraged in Hebrews to practice this daily so that we won't be deceived and harden our hearts.

In a world that has plenty of hardened hearts, I encourage you moms to soften your heart before the Father. We need truthful encouragement to sharpen us each day. Teach your kids to keep soft hearts before God and others. One way to do this is to find a God-loving local church community. I know from personal experience that looking for a church community can be very challenging and daunting. But if you keep asking the Lord and don't give up in the search, I believe that God will be faithful to answer your prayers. Of course no church is perfect, but neither are we!

When Chris and I were looking for a local church to plug in to, God spoke to me about considering our family's core values when looking for a church. We thought of a few core values and this was very helpful in guiding our church searching process. With each church we attended, whether it be for a few weeks or months, we would later line it up to those values and see if it was a good match for our family.

God is so kind in speaking to us, His beloved children. He did not design us for community, just to hide community from you. Keep asking Him and keep searching for a church that is a good fit for your family to thrive and grow in Him.

I invite you to pray this prayer today:

Dear Heavenly Father,
Thank You for creating us for community. Please help us to find a local church family that aligns with our core values. Help us when we get discouraged and encourage us by confirming what church we should commit to.
In Jesus' name, Amen.

DAY 40

Overwhelming Circumstances

The wife of a man from the company of the prophets cried out to Elisha, "Your servant my husband is dead, and you know that he revered the Lord. But now his creditor is coming to take my two boys as his slaves." Elisha replied to her, "How can I help you? Tell me, what do you have in your house?" "Your servant has nothing there at all," she said, "except a small jar of olive oil."Elisha said, "Go around and ask all your neighbors for empty jars. Don't ask for just a few. Then go inside and shut the door behind you and your sons. Pour oil into all the jars, and as each is filled, put it to one side."She left him and shut the door behind her and her sons. They brought the jars to her and she kept pouring. When all the jars were full, she said to her son, "Bring me another one."But he replied, "There is not a jar left." Then the oil stopped flowing.She went and told the man of God, and he said, "Go, sell the oil and pay your debts. You and your sons can live on what is left."

2 KINGS 4:1-7

Something the Lord has continuously challenged me in my life is trusting in His provision. Time and time again I am reminded of my own fickleness, my lack of faith, and my doubts of His goodness and character.

Yesterday I felt so encouraged again by this scripture.

Many, if not all of us, in the whole world are going through uncertain times after the pandemic. Whether it's concerning unstable health, virus fears, unknown financial future, strained relationships, loneliness, or housing, the list can go on and on for so many of us. The widow in this passage lost her husband and if that was not horrible enough, she was in a desperate situation, about to lose her two sons.

Do you ever feel cornered by your circumstances too?

I have felt cornered at times in my life – thankfully never to the extreme of this widow – but sometimes life's circumstances can make me feel completely overwhelmed. I love how the Lord shows us that there is always a way out when we cry out to Him and place our worry and trust in His hands. Often, His answer may not be the answer we want. I'm just being honest: if I was this mother, my initial reaction would have been annoyance, asking God to give me actual cash to quickly pay the debts. Why was Elisha talking about empty jars at this critical, desperate time?!

But the Lord had a different plan. He wanted to provide for this woman in a different, completely out of the box way, a miracle that would blow her mind. In a sense maybe He was asking, "Will you take one step of faith and trust me, even though you don't fully understand why I am asking this of you, and you don't know the end result?"

If you currently feel "cornered" or overwhelmed by life's circumstances, I want to encourage you to look to our good Father for your provision and answer. Stories like this reveal that He is always faithful to His beloved ones. He may answer you in a completely unconventional and different way than you may consider ideal, but I truly have faith that He will indeed answer you when you cry out.

I have countless stories from our lives where we have seen the provision of the Lord come through for us, even at times when we have been unwise with our money and didn't "deserve" to get bailed out by the Lord. But God is good to us even when we don't "deserve it" or "earn it."

I feel like I should share a more serious story here, but the one I thought of is a funny one; funny because it shows how short-sighted and immature we were when we were newlyweds. You can have a good laugh at Chris and I today.

We found out we were pregnant with our first child in our second month of marriage. It was a time of uncertainty and wonder, but one thing we did know is that we wanted to do something fun together before our baby came. We had a two-week window between him finishing his seminary classes and his actual graduation day. So we decided to take a cross-country road trip from our little apartment in New Jersey to visit his sister in California! Without much planning, a full tank of gas, an atlas, and a Motel 6 directory, we ventured off on our very first road trip in our marriage.

Somewhere in between New Mexico and Arizona, our air conditioning knob broke. This is a first-world problem, but definitely inconvenient since we still had to drive through some super-hot states and I was pregnant! When we finally made it to my sister-in-law's apartment, we had a fun time exploring San Francisco with her and eating wonderful food. Chris took the car in to a mechanic to get the broken knob replaced. But he got a grim call from the mechanic shortly after. The mechanic saw our license plate from New Jersey and said, "You aren't planning to drive this car back to New Jersey, are you? Because you will break down on the way unless you make some urgent repairs." Both of our parents were going to be excitedly waiting for us at his graduation. My parents used to own a store and they *never* closed their store except for graduations and weddings of immediate family members. Chris' graduation from seminary was a huge deal for both of our parents, so we could not miss it!

What else could this broke seminary couple do with an unexpected $2,000 repair? We had zero savings and only enough money to make it back home, so we charged the car repairs on our credit card and finished our road trip with a cloud of new debt hanging over our heads, but we made it just in time for his graduation. The morning of Chris' graduation, a friend congratulated him for an award he was going to receive at the ceremony. Chris was shocked because he was unaware that he was getting any awards. It was from a class he loved, so he felt really honored. But then his friend said, "This isn't just a certificate...they give you money!"

When Chris opened the award envelope, we were shocked to see a check for $3,000! Our parents didn't understand why Chris and I began jumping up and down like crazy people. We obviously had not yet told them about the fresh debt we accrued on our trip, but now we had enough to pay it all off. We got to share the exciting news with them afterwards at dinner. Chris and I grew up together and matured a lot those beginning years of marriage. Thinking about this story still cracks me up.

Honestly, most of our debt was not resolved in such a quick miraculous way. In fact, most of our other debts were paid one step at a time. God definitely uses wise financial planning as well. This is just one funny story from our lives of His provision. We have miracle stories as well as stories of normal hard work and budgeting...but I just wanted to encourage you with a good laugh today.

I invite you to pray this prayer today:

Dear Heavenly Father,
Thank You for always watching over me. I give You every circumstance that is overwhelming me. I trust You with every area in my life, including my finances. Please provide for all of my needs.
In Jesus' name, Amen.

DAY 41

Unique

For just as each of us has one body with many members, and these members do not all have the same function, so in Christ we, though many, form one body, and each member belongs to all the others. We have different gifts, according to the grace given to each of us.

ROMANS 12:4-6A

As moms, we have been entrusted with such a precious and valuable gift in our children. Each of them is so unique and wonderful and created in God's perfect timing. God chose YOU out of all the women in the entire world to be your precious child's mother. That is an incredible invitation handed to us by God our Father.

I believe one of our roles as moms is to identify our children's gifts and encourage them to use them for God's glory. As we celebrate their giftings, this will help inspire them to see the Lord's Hand in their lives. Why did He give them this unique gift and how can it be used for His glory?

Each of my kids have been made so distinctly different in God's design. My eldest son is a gifted leader and worship leader.

Growing up, his siblings and kids on the playground would always follow him around and look to him for leadership. I see more evidence of this now at his college Christian fellowship where his leadership gift is being utilized daily. I found it fascinating that even in his freshman year, older students would ask him for advice and help.

Another son is an incredible artist and has such a brilliant mind. He has been leading people in creativity since he was three years old! He would envision these innovative crafts for his siblings and other kids to follow and he would teach them how to make them. He is also the artist that drew the cover of this book. I love it and I am glad he agreed to do it!

My third son has such a tender heart and is amazing with serving others. He feels called to become a pediatrician because he wants to help children who are sick like he was when he was born prematurely. People love him wherever he goes and I am proud of his desire to help others.

My first daughter is sweet and a wonderful artist. She doesn't know yet how the Lord will use her gifts, but I believe that He will show her as she grows older. Our youngest is a budding artist as well. She brings life and joy to any room that she is in.

Each of my kids is so unique. Their various gifts and talents are also vastly different. As a mother, it would be wrong to try to force them down a path that God didn't create them to be on. I believe that it is our privilege as moms to call out the gifts that God has placed in our kids, affirm them, and help them flourish in them. And when they are called to leave the "nest" of our home, God will be faithful to continue leading them in His great love and wisdom.

I invite you to pray this prayer today:

Dear Heavenly Father,
Please help my kids to know You for themselves, deep in each of their hearts. Let them know Jesus as their Lord and Savior. I pray that You would help me to see the gifts that

You have placed in my kids. Please give me divine wisdom to lead them in the path that You have set out before them. In Jesus' name, Amen.

DAY 42

Discipline and Guidance

Endure hardship as discipline; God is treating you as his children. For what children are not disciplined by their father? If you are not disciplined – and everyone undergoes discipline – then you are not legitimate, not true sons and daughters at all. Moreover, we have all had human fathers who disciplined us and we respected them for it. How much more should we submit to the Father of spirits and live! They disciplined us for a little while as they thought best; but God disciplines us for our good, in order that we may share in his holiness. No discipline seems pleasant at the time, but painful. Later on, however, it produces a harvest of righteousness and peace for those who have been trained by it.

HEBREWS 12:7-11

Parenting comes with so many challenges, and learning how to discipline our kids appropriately is one of the hardest things we had to learn. Each child has such a unique personality and bent. I believe as parents it is our privilege and responsibility to learn about how God made each of our kids differently and to guide them accordingly. Godly discipline, not done in anger, is necessary for our kids and homes to thrive. One of the fruits of the Spirit is self-control

(Galatians 5:22-23). Godly discipline requires self-control on the part of the parents and that is something crucial to keep in mind.

My oldest sister gave me some excellent advice when my first son was born when I was asking her for baby sleep advice. She said, "Eunice, he is not a robot. Each kid is different." I know that this shouldn't be mind-blowing advice, but as a new mom, honestly it was! As each additional child came, I remembered her wise words not only in the area of sleep but also in the area of discipline and guiding my kids along their own individual paths.

If you have more than one child, you know that some kids respond to a stern "no" from a parent when disobeying. Other kids might look at you and laugh when you say "no" and they might need some other forms of discipline. I cannot say this enough but God made each child so unique! We as parents have a wonderful responsibility to teach and admonish our kids to be responsible adults, ones who understand submission, ones who are have thankful hearts, ones who understand how to live for God in this dark and sinful world.

With God all things are possible. Do not lose heart and give up in disciplining and guiding your kids in the ways of the Lord.

I invite you to pray this prayer today:

Dear Heavenly Father,
Please show me how uniquely You made each of my kids.
Help me to guide and discipline them according to how
You want them to grow. I offer each of my children to
You. Thank You that godly discipline will reap a harvest
of righteousness and peace for our household.
In Jesus' name, Amen.

DAY 43

Good Gifts

Every good and perfect gift is from above, coming down from the Father of the heavenly lights, who does not change like shifting shadows. He chose to give us birth through the word of truth, that we might be a kind of firstfruits of all he created.

JAMES 1:17-18

I believe that teaching our kids about thankfulness and stewardship is critical for our children to thrive as people. Where do all good gifts come from? Our Heavenly Father. If adults or children don't know this, they will become spoiled and entitled.

Thankfulness and an understanding of stewarding our belongings and money well are all lessons I believe parents can teach their kids starting at a young age. Beginning from when they are toddlers, we can teach our kids how to put away their toys, to not throw things, and to say please and thank you. I believe this helps teach our children thankfulness. One thing Chris and I have done is to teach our kids to tithe when they get gifts on their birthday or other occasions. We wanted them to understand that everything comes from God, to be grateful, and to manage their things well.

Teaching our kids how to be thankful and good stewards is one way that I believe we as Christians stand out in this dark world. Wouldn't you say it is refreshing when you meet kids that are kind, polite, and thankful? And then you wonder what their parents did to raise them in this way? Let people wonder and then you can share with them about God!

A time that awakened my heart to thankfulness on a whole new level was when we moved to the Middle East. There was an ongoing war in a neighboring country when we arrived. There were refugees lined up and down every street our family walked on in that great city. Moms with babies and toddlers would sit on cardboard boxes, rain or shine, begging for money or food. The Lord kept asking me to picture myself sitting on that box with my kids. Would I want someone to notice us? It was absolutely heartbreaking and I gained a life-changing perspective that I know marked my kids' hearts as well. Picturing yourself walking in someone else's shoes is a great way to form both compassion and gratitude in our hearts.

Moms, today if you are struggling with thankfulness, I encourage you to picture yourself walking in someone else's shoes. This is a spiritual exercise that helps us remember where all of our good gifts come from! Praise God today for the blessings in your life. This is a great exercise you can do with your kids as well.

I invite you to pray this prayer today:

Dear Heavenly Father,
Thank You for every single one of Your good gifts in my life. Help me to be a good steward of the gifts You have given to me, starting with my children and home. I love You Lord. Thank You for loving me first. I choose gratitude today. In Jesus' name, Amen.

DAY 44

Dignity and Worth

So God created mankind in his own image,
in the image of God he created them;
male and female he created them.

GENESIS 1:27

Did you know that each one of us was made in the image of God? That means that we were created with innate dignity and worth. Being in Christ also means that we do not have to earn our value or prove ourselves to others. But because we live in a fallen world, most of us grow up with false messages about where our value or worth come from, which leads many to have low self-esteem.

My growth the area of self-esteem didn't happen overnight. It was a journey that I had to lean into. A healing process may be painful but is always worth it. I started walking in a new level of confidence when I realized deep in my heart and spirit the answer to this question,

"Who is the one who gives me my dignity and self-worth?"

It's God! He created each of us so uniquely on purpose. He

does not make mistakes. And He did not make a mistake in creating you. My worth does not rely on man's opinions, how much money we have in the bank, how big and tidy my house is, how well other people might think my kids behave, how many organic foods we eat in our diet, if I can still fit into my clothes from ten years ago, etc. None of these are bad things, they just aren't what my worth should depend on because they are ever changing.

If we don't find our dignity and worth in Christ, we will look for it in other places. When we find our confidence in Christ, we can pour out to our kids in a whole manner and help them find their identity in Him as well.

I invite you to pray this prayer today:

Dear Heavenly Father,
Thank You for who You made me. Thank You for making me unique on purpose. Please forgive me for any ways I have hated things about myself (list any ways that come to mind). I choose to find my identity and value in YOU. Please heal me in this area and show me Your truth of who You created me to be today and every day.
In Jesus' name, Amen.

DAY 45

Kingdom Values

Do not love the world or anything in the world. If anyone loves the world, love for the Father is not in them. For everything in the world – the lust of the flesh, the lust of the eyes, and the pride of life – comes not from the Father but from the world. The world and its desires pass away, but whoever does the will of God lives forever.

1 JOHN 2:15-17

As parents, one of our God-given privileges is to teach our kids to love the things that God loves and hate the things that God hates. This is one of the ways that our families and kids will be world changers. We will change the atmosphere in our neighborhoods and communities by loving God and holding on to the values He establishes from the Bible.

When our kids see us walk in forgiveness and reconciliation the way that the Bible teaches it, they will see a different path than what the world teaches. The world tells us to take revenge, hold on to bitterness, they don't deserve forgiveness, and to fight for your own rights. I saw my parents walk in this Christ-like way throughout my childhood. When I was young, I was so angry when they were treated unjustly at their store by customers and then they would tell me they didn't fight back because they wanted to walk like Jesus did. It would infuriate me as a child and teen, but now that I am older and a more mature believer, I am grateful for their example. The way they responded to certain situations was not passivity like I thought when I was young. It was a choice of humility and Christ-likeness and I am proud of them and grateful for the example they set for me.

When our kids see us tithe and give generously, and we talk and discuss values like generosity with them, they see a Biblical value rather than hoarding things for ourselves. We as God's people give because He is so generous to us and we are just stewards of what He has given us.

When our kids see us reading the Bible or when we read the Bible to them, when they see us praying or when we pray together with them, when our kids see us worshipping the Lord through the different seasons and circumstances of life, these things make an impact in their hearts, minds, and spirits.

God is so so good in giving us these beautiful blessings in our home. Let us lead by example in our homes and teach them faithfully about Him every day.

I invite you to pray this prayer today:

Dear Heavenly Father,
Please teach me how to love the things that You love and hate the things that You hate. Please transform my thinking and make me more like Christ. Please give me the grace and wisdom to teach my kids how to love You and love the things that You love and hate the things that You hate. In Jesus' name, Amen.

DAY 46

Squelch Sibling Rivalry

Now Israel loved Joseph more than any of his other sons, because he had been born to him in his old age; and he made an ornate robe for him. When his brothers saw that their father loved him more than any of them, they hated him and could not speak a kind word to him.

GENESIS 37:3-4

I believe giving our kids siblings (if at all possible) is one of the greatest gifts we can give them. I am talking about siblings both adopted and biologically related. I am blessed to have both and my sisters are a huge gift that my parents gave me.

I am the youngest of four daughters. Growing up my mom would always say, "Your sisters are your best friends." When I was a child and teen, I always thought that was annoying, especially when we were fighting, but I always say the same thing to my kids now. I am grateful for each of my sisters and for my mom who set that vision before us.

We are sinful beings and we need Jesus' sanctification in other to build healthy relationships. Encouraging sibling rivalry is poison to a family. A value I hold tightly in my parenting is this: do not compare your children to other people, including each other. Do you like being compared to other people? I hate it because comparison is toxic. It distracts you from who God made you to be and it causes insecurity in our personhood.

When my kids bicker and fight, I always remind them like my mom did, "I know this is hard now, but just remember that they are your best friends. They will be with you through every season of your life." This is so annoying to hear when you are arguing with a sibling, but it is important to cast that vision to our kids. Our children need to know that God has made them each a son and daughter of the Most High God. They never have to compare themselves to others and we as parents certainly never have justification to do the same. Love them unconditionally the way that God has loved you.

I invite you to pray this prayer today:

Dear Heavenly Father,
Thank You so much for making each of my children so uniquely and wonderfully. Help me to see and call out the character qualities and gifts You have given to each of them. I pray that my kids would walk in unity and friendship with one another. Let them champion each other in who You made each of them to be. In Jesus' name, Amen.

DAY 47

Renewed Hope

But as for me, I watch in hope for the Lord, I wait for God my Savior; my God will hear me.

MICAH 7:7

Hope is something that this world needs more of. A myriad of things can cause us to lose hope: when you read the news, when unwanted circumstances come crashing around you, when a job is lost, when a loved one passes away, when an investment tanks, or when sickness comes.

But for the people of God, our hope and trust are found in Him, not our circumstances. When we rely on Him when things are crashing down around us, it is a testimony to this dark world. The world needs hope and we as the people of God need to find our strength and hope in Him daily.

There is an author that resides in Colorado Springs that I greatly admire, but she is hardly home because she is often traveling around the world for her ministry. I have read several of her books and listen to her podcasts regularly. One time, I was in a very emotionally challenging season. I love celebrations and

I love the idea of whole birthday weeks. I usually enjoy meeting up with girlfriends when it's my birthday and we also have a family dinner. Chris and the kids make me feel very loved and celebrated. But my birthday came around that year and I had no friends nearby to celebrate with me. (This is definitely one of the challenging parts about moving a lot).

The morning of my birthday, I got a text from a random acquaintance that I had not spoken with in a whole year. I had met this friendly mom at our previous homeschool co-op. She wrote, "Your favorite author is coming to my small group tonight. This is not a public invitation, but I wanted to invite you because God reminded me of you this morning. I remembered how much you love her." My jaw literally dropped. I immediately wrote back and told her how much I would love to come and how this felt like a birthday gift straight from heaven.

How did this mom acquaintance remember me after a full year of not talking or seeing each other if the Lord hadn't whispered my name to her that morning? I had a wonderful time at that small group, meeting that author on my birthday. That precious mom bought me a copy of the author's latest book and asked her to sign it for me as a birthday gift. When I got in my car after the meeting, I bawled my eyes out the entire way home. I was completely blown away and in awe of God. It felt like the Lord kissed me with a renewed hope and said, "Eunice, I see you in this hard season." I knew he worked a miracle for me orchestrating that night and I felt so loved and seen by Him.

God is trustworthy. He is kind. He is faithful. He is able to give you hope in the hard seasons.

I invite you to pray this prayer today:

Dear Heavenly Father,
I put my trust in You again. I will not lose hope because of my circumstances. I choose to hope in You today. Please fill me with Your Holy Spirit and renew my hope.
In Jesus' name, Amen.

DAY 48

His Delight

The Lord your God is with you, the Mighty Warrior who saves. He will take great delight in you; in his love he will no longer rebuke you, but will rejoice over you with singing.

ZEPHANIAH 3:17

Did you know that the Father takes great DELIGHT in you? Delight is not a neutral, indifferent feeling. When you delight in something, there is joy, there is gladness, there is overwhelming happiness! That is how the Father feels about each one of us.

One time our church called a fast for twenty-one days. I decided to do a Daniel Fast for spiritual breakthrough. A few days into the fast, I ended up at the dentist with throbbing pain in my mouth. It turns out that my gums had an infection. Shortly after this, the day before I was scheduled to record a video announcement for church, I dropped something on my mouth and busted my lip; it immediately started bleeding and swelling! About a week later, my body broke out in full body hives for some unknown reason and I had to go to urgent care for medication. I was worried that the hives would cover my face because I was leading a prayer meeting in a few days. The hives went away the morning of that prayer meeting and thankfully they never reached my face. In addition to all of these things, I got a sinus infection out of nowhere! All of these random circumstances back-to-back really got on my nerves. I felt like the devil was just trying to discourage me during my fast and sadly some days, it worked!

While I was beginning to recover from my annoying hives, I got a beautiful package in the mail. My good friend sent me a gorgeous new leather purse and matching wallet. She wrote me a sweet card inside. It said that she felt the Lord wanted her to gift this to me to remind me that He is going to take care of our family's needs *and* wants.

Honestly, when I got her encouraging package, I felt like the Lord was just smiling over me with His kindness. It took me many years to realize that He delights over me, just like He delights in all His children. I hope that this testimony reminds you that He delights over you too. This is not just a blessing for some individuals, this is a reality for all of us who have given our lives to Him.

I invite you to pray this prayer today:

Dear Heavenly Father,
Thank You for creating me. Thank You for delighting in me. Please show me how You see me and let me actually believe it in my spirit. In Jesus' name, Amen.

DAY 49

He Carries Us Through

The Sovereign Lord is my strength; he makes my feet like the feet of a deer, he enables me to tread on the heights.

HABAKKUK 3:19

God is able to make you flourish and grow even in weak and uncertain places. I believe motherhood exposes all of our strengths and weaknesses. After I gave birth to each of our babies, an incredible feeling of accomplishment overcame me. It was exhilarating to see the face of my baby after carrying him or her all those months. I have had the privilege to welcome home adoptive parents from their overseas travels when picking up their children from other countries and I experienced that same feeling of elation. The mountains of paperwork and red tape had been overcome, visas were approved, and finally their children were home with them. It's a beautiful picture to witness as everyone rejoices!

But once that initial adrenaline rush subsides and normal life resumes, our weaknesses are totally exposed. I never realized how selfish I was until I became a parent of a newborn. I never realized how unsure of myself I was until I became a mom. I never felt as powerless as I did when I was trying to nurse my babies but my body didn't physically produce enough milk for them to thrive. (After my third child, I finally found out from a lactation consultant that I had a medical condition that delayed my milk production for every child. I had seen four or five different lactation consultants at that point in my life that had no idea what was wrong with me, but that is another story for a different day).

Even though all of my weaknesses were exposed when I became a mom, I definitely can testify that God helped me through every hard patch and he is still helping me every day.

It's in these hard places, that we can testify: God is my strength! He is bringing me through! He is enabling me to survive and thrive! He is securing my footing so I can tread on these heights. Moms, keep giving your weaknesses to Him, and He will give you a testimony if you keep pushing through.

I invite you to pray this prayer today:

Dear Heavenly Father,
Thank You for being my strength. I give You all of my weaknesses (list all the places you feel weak and give it to Him). I know that You are going to give me a testimony to share with others when I overcome these challenges. Thank You Lord!
In Jesus' name, Amen.

DAY 50

Restoration

I will repay you for the years the locusts have eaten — the great locust and the young locust, the other locusts and the locust swarm — my great army that I sent among you. You will have plenty to eat, until you are full, and you will praise the name of the Lord your God, who has worked wonders for you; never again will my people be shamed. Then you will know that I am in Israel, that I am the Lord your God, and that there is no other; never again will my people be shamed.

JOEL 2:25-27

God is our provider. Over and over again in scripture He makes this clear. When I was a young mom, I wrongly believed that my husband is the provider, so I would look to Chris in unhealthy ways in expectation for him to provide. But as I learned more in the scriptures that while God uses our husbands to provide for our families, He is the ultimate source of our provision.

There are times in our lives that we may go through challenging financial circumstances, but if we look to God, He is the one who will not only provide but make a way for things that the enemy stole from us to be given back to us. If we are faithful in our tithes and offerings, I do believe that the Lord will hear our prayers and restore that which was lost.

When you feel like financial resources have been lost or even stolen from you, ask God to repay you for those years that the locusts have eaten.

This may not happen overnight, but I believe it can and will happen if we keep asking the Lord and look to Him for our provision. One time our family's income was cut in half due to unexpected circumstances. Initially, this shock was incredibly challenging, but then Chris and I repeatedly chose to trust in the Lord to not only provide but pay back what we felt the enemy had taken from us. Over two years passed and through a miraculous selling of our home, the Lord paid us back in that one transaction double the amount we lost in those two years. It was amazing and we are so grateful to God for His kindness and generosity to our family.

If you have been in a similar circumstance where you have felt that the enemy has robbed you in some area, ask God to pay it back to you. Keep asking Him. This may not happen overnight, but if you do not give up hope and keep asking, I believe that the Lord will answer your prayers.

I invite you to pray this prayer today:

Dear Heavenly Father,
I choose to forgive (name the person or circumstance that you feel like stole from you). I release them into the freedom of my forgiveness. Today, I ask that You would repay whatever the enemy has stolen from my life.
In Jesus' name, Amen.

DAY 51

Storms

The Lord is good, a refuge in times of trouble.
He cares for those who trust in him...

NAHUM 1:7

Have you ever been in a season where life seems completely out of your control and your back is up against a wall? In those times turn to Him. In those times worship Him. Behold who God is and let Him be your refuge.

My third child was born in another state when my husband was on a work trip and I accompanied him with our two little ones. Zach was thirty-five weeks gestation when he was born and his lungs were not fully developed yet. I went into preterm labor just hours before we were supposed to get on our flight home. Chris and I didn't want to wake up our one and two-year-old unnecessarily if I was only experiencing false labor like my midwife thought, so I labored in the hotel bathroom for four hours in denial that I was in active labor before I knew something was not right.

Chris grabbed our two sleeping children and we got in the car and drove to the hospital at 5 a.m. with our kids screaming the whole way from being rudely awakened in the middle of the night. As soon as we got to the emergency room, they told me that I was ten millimeters dilated and it was time to push. And just like that, our baby Zachariah came into the world. Zach had to be hospitalized and was in the neonatal intensive care unit for ten days until he could breathe on his own.

I am so deeply grateful to all the doctors and nurses that God used to save my son's life. There is no feeling more helpless and powerless than when your child's life is completely out of your hands. All we could do during that time is lean on the Lord for strength and plead to Him for Zach's life. We had family and friends in different states praying for us and God answered our desperate prayers and Zach lived. He is the tallest of all of our children and has never had lung problems since. Praise God!

God is a good Father. Sadly, I know that not everyone who has a sick child gets the same answer we got when Zach was discharged in good health from the hospital, but I do know that God cares for those who trust in Him. Look for refuge in Him for I know that He can comfort you through any storm you are facing.

I invite you to pray this prayer today:

***Dear Heavenly Father,
Thank You that You are my refuge in times of trouble. I choose to put my trust in You. I give You this storm I am facing (name the storm and surrender it to Him).
In Jesus' name, Amen.***

DAY 52

Obey Him

Does the Lord delight in burnt offerings and sacrifices as much as in obeying the Lord? To obey is better than sacrifice, and to heed is better than the fat of rams.

1 SAMUEL 15:22B

Has there ever been a time that the Lord prompted you to do something but you didn't do it? I have, and I have had to repent when He kindly reminds me of these times.

In the last months that we lived abroad, the Lord told me during a church service to write my first ebook, "A Walk On the Water." When he clearly put the idea on my heart, I told him, "Lord, I will not write a book. Can't you see I am very busy taking care of my five kids that you gave me and homeschooling them?" He immediately replied, "Eunice, your friend Sara just wrote her first book and homeschools her six kids." I paused, and after I thought more about it, I had to laugh because He was right. Sara had just released her first book and I was amazed how she had carved out the time to write it.

Initially I did not want to obey Him because writing a book takes a lot of discipline, thought, and vulnerability. I was pretty content just vegging out each night. But I had walked with the Lord long enough to know that I should at least try to obey Him, so I responded and said, "Lord, if you really want me to do this, please give me the strength and desire to do it." The Lord immediately started downloading ideas into my head about how to write it out and he told me that He wanted me to give it away for free.

Shortly after this, Chris was going on a two-week trip of pastoral visits to strengthen and encourage the missionaries in our organization. It was unusual for him to be gone that long, because he would typically travel for a week at the longest. God put the idea (and desire) in my heart to write every evening while Chris was gone. I plugged away each night at my short book and by the time Chris came home, my rough draft was complete.

I am so thankful for this book for many reasons. This book has encouraged more people than I ever thought it could in both gaining a heart for overseas missions and in overcoming fear. But mostly, I am thankful I wrote this book because it is our family's testimony of how God called us to move to the Middle East for those three and a half years. I am not good at journaling and although I thought I would never forget a lot of the stories in my little book, I realized when rereading it years later, that I indeed forgot many of the testimonies I wrote down in there. God is so wise and He knows us better than we know ourselves! Writing "A Walk On the Water" also gave me the courage to begin this book when the Lord asked me to. Instead of responding to Him with an ungrateful attitude, this time I immediately said, "Lord, please just help me to write it."

Is the Lord inviting you to obey Him in something today? I encourage you to say "yes" to Him and do not delay in taking steps forward.

I invite you to pray this prayer today:

Dear Heavenly Father,
Thank You for speaking to me. Please give me the desire and strength to obey You when You invite me to do something. Give me the grace and the ideas to move forward in obedience.
In Jesus' name, Amen.

DAY 53

Generational God

Know therefore that the Lord your God is God; he is the faithful God, keeping his covenant of love to a thousand generations of those who love him and keep his commandments.

DEUTERONOMY 7:9

God is a generational God. He is so generous in blessing the generations that follow us just because of our obedience. He is faithful in remembering everything we have offered to Him.

Chris' paternal grandmother is an incredible example of this. Although I have never had the privilege to meet her because she passed away when Chris was in middle school, I have heard many stories about her. She was an extraordinary, strong Christian woman. She lived during the Korean War and endured many hardships during that time. When the war broke out and borders were rapidly redrawn, she was separated from her husband because he was in a different town on business and was not allowed to return to the family. Her oldest two children were also not living at home at the time, so she was left alone to raise her other four children, ages thirteen to one. When the South Korean Army urged willing citizens to move to the south and provided transportation, she had the courage to leave her hometown with her four young children in tow. I am crying even as I type this, thinking of the sacrifices she made to give her children a better future.

Today, North Korean Christians go through such intense persecution under their government and it is horribly sad that many people are still suffering there to this day. I can't imagine what would have happened to Chris' family if his grandma hadn't made the brave choices she made and I am eternally grateful. She was a wonderful woman of faith and she passed this faith down to my father-in-law and mother-in-law and she committed Chris to the work of the ministry when he was a young child. Chris' parents have been an incredible blessing in my life and I am so grateful to have married into this godly family. They have experienced tremendous heartaches in their lives, but their love and faith in God is inspiring. I am so thankful for the generational blessing that has come down to all of us from Chris' grandma's obedience and sacrifice in following the Lord.

Moms, we do not know what our choices today will mean to the generations that follow after us. I pray that as we walk closely with the Lord, He will give us a greater vision for our future generations. If you did not come from a Christian home, please take heart because as you live for Jesus now, you are causing new generational blessings to flow down your family line. You will be the curse breaker and you will leave a legacy of loving God to the future generations.

I invite you to pray this prayer today:

Dear Heavenly Father,
Thank You that You are a God who loves every generation and legacy. I pray that every generational curse in my family line would be broken off in the name of Jesus. I ask that every

generational blessing in my family line will flow in Jesus' mighty name. Please teach me how to leave a godly legacy for my children and their children and the generations that may follow. In Jesus' name, Amen.

DAY 54

Breaking Generational Curses

This is what the Lord Almighty says: "Return to me," declares the Lord Almighty, "and I will return to you," says the Lord Almighty. Do not be like your ancestors, to whom the earlier prophets proclaimed: This is what the Lord Almighty says: "Turn from your evil ways and your evil practices." But they would not listen or pay attention to me, declares the Lord. Where are your ancestors now? And the prophets, do they live forever? But did not my words and my decrees, which I commanded my servants the prophets, overtake your ancestors? Then they repented and said, "The Lord Almighty has done to us what our ways and practices deserve, just as he determined to do."

ZECHARIAH 1:3B-6

Isn't it incredible that in Christ we are able to cut off sin patterns and break generational curses from our families? My dad grew up with a non-Christian, alcoholic father. But when he married my mom and they started their family, they decided to break the generational curse of alcohol addiction and rarely brought alcohol into our home. I am so thankful that they took this sin pattern seriously and chose to walk with Christ and break this sin off of our family line.

We as parents can repent to the Lord and choose to stop the sinful patterns that have affected our families for generations because of Jesus' blood. God promises in this scripture that if we return to Him, He will respond and return to us. Isn't that amazing? His grace is stunning. It is an incredible promise to us, His people.

Maybe your mom or dad had rage issues and you see them cropping up in your own parenting. You can repent and ask the Lord to deliver your family from that sin pattern. Maybe your parents had ungodly beliefs about money (this can happen whether you are rich or poor) and you need to break agreement with that in Jesus' name. Maybe someone in your family line had an addiction like my grandfather; you can cut that off of your family line today with God's help. Ask Him to lead you and seek a godly Christian counselor if you need to. Even if you are the first Christian in your entire family line, God can help you establish a godly family if you ask Him. He just needs one willing heart in your family and you can choose to be that one!

I invite you to pray this prayer today:

Dear Heavenly Father,
Thank You for the promise that if I return to You, You will return to me. Please forgive me for my sin and the sins of my family line (name the sins that you feel need to be repented for now). I choose to return to You Lord. I ask that the blood of Jesus would break these sinful generational patterns in my family line. Cleanse me of our sins Lord and build a godly family through me.
In Jesus' name, Amen.

DAY 55

God's Timing

There is a time for everything, and a season for every activity under the heavens...He has made everything beautiful in its time. He has also set eternity in the human heart; yet no one can fathom what God has done from beginning to end.

ECCLESIASTES 3:1, 11

God's ways are not our ways. His timing is not our timing. Our times and seasons are in His Hands. God gave your beautiful child or children in His perfect timing. You are blessed to be your child's parent in this exact moment in time. He chose YOU and God does not make mistakes.

God chose you to love your unique child and to teach your children about His ways. God has purposed this motherhood season in your life when all of your kids are under one roof, to be a blessing to you and to them. I know that there are hard, challenging days, but ask Him how to use each day for His glory.

Timing is a funny thing if you pause to think about it. There were many years in my life that I could not sit down to even enjoy a book and now here I am writing one. Many moms with young kids look at me and exclaim, "Eunice! I don't know how you juggle it all!" And I have to remind them, "Seasons change and my kids are more independent now. There does come a day when your child will be able to pour their own water, make their own breakfast, and cook themselves lunch. I sleep through the night almost every night and now there is space for me to make my podcasts. I have time to both read and write, and you will have more time and space in the future too." This day might not arrive tomorrow, but it will indeed come before you know it.

Do not compare your individual season with other moms in your life or from social media. Use God's word and voice to guide and direct you and your family each day of your lives and He will be faithful to lead you. He will carry you through every season if you commit your plans to Him.

I invite you to pray this prayer today:

Dear Heavenly Father,
Thank You that our times are in Your hands. You are a good Father and I trust You to work everything out for my good in YOUR time, not mine. Please help me to keep eternity in my heart and live for eternal things that don't waste away and help me to teach my kids to do the same.
In Jesus' name, Amen.

DAY 56

Mother Deborah

Villagers in Israel would not fight; they held back until I, Deborah, arose, until I arose, a mother in Israel.

JUDGES 5:7

I love Deborah in the Bible. I have always felt provoked by and drawn to her story of courage. She was a leader of the Israelites, a judge, and a prophet. She led the Israelites into battle. The Lord commanded Barak to go and fight, but he refused to go unless Deborah went with them. Deborah accompanied them and they were victorious in battle.

I find it fascinating that in Deborah's song in Judges 5:7, she does not call herself a judge or a prophet or the leader of Israel; she calls herself a "mother." Of all the titles Deborah could have chosen, she calls herself a "mother in Israel."

Why is that? Could it be because mothers have a different courage when it comes to saving their children from destruction? A bully will not mess with a mother's fierce love because she will send them running. A Christian mother will pray forth the destiny on their children's lives more than anyone.

We love our children and will do whatever it takes for them to thrive. That's why I believe Deborah was the right leader for Israel at that time. She was prophetic, discerning, courageous, bold, and willing to die for her children's (the people of Israel) destiny.

I believe God is calling forth each one of you beautiful moms to be a "Deborah" for your family. Moms who will courageously be raising your children as disciples of Christ in the warmth of your homes. You will host people in your homes and people will notice that you are living differently as you let the light of Christ shine brightly through your hospitality. You will make brave choices for your family in faith, knowing that even if it's scary, your family will obey God above the norms of this world. You will pray and fight in the Spirit over your children's salvation and the destiny and callings that God has purposed over their lives. I believe in you dear momma!

I invite you to pray this prayer today:

Dear Heavenly Father,
Thank You for heroes of faith like Deborah. Please give me courage for the battles I have to fight. Help me teach my kids to live fearlessly and to walk in faith.
In Jesus' name, Amen.

DAY 57

Choices

See, I set before you today life and prosperity, death and destruction. For I command you today to love the Lord your God, to walk in obedience to him, and to keep his commands, decrees and laws; then you will live and increase, and the Lord your God will bless you in the land you are entering to possess.

DEUTERONOMY 30:15-16

I love that God empowers us with the gift of choice. When I was a young person, I used to hate it. I wished that God would just decide things for me and tell me what to do. "Wouldn't life be easier like that?" I always wondered. But as I have gotten older, I realize free will is a gift. God could have just created robots, but He didn't want people who are forced to love and obey Him. Who wants a robotic husband who feels trapped in their marriage and doesn't really want to be with you? No one.

We all long for genuine love, but true love is a choice. God is longing for our love but he won't force us to follow Him. When we choose to obey Him, we demonstrate our love and commitment to Him.

God is longing for families who will lay everything down at

His feet, in complete love and devotion. Ones who will go against the grain of the world's ways and follow Him to the cross daily. As a mom, there are so many opportunities to go to the cross every day: when you need alone time, but you choose to read your Bible and spend some minutes with God instead; when you don't want to change another poopy diaper and you want to yell at your spouse to come do it, but you choose to serve your family once again instead; when you just want to sleep but your baby is crying to be nursed again, so you get up to feed your child; when your multiple kids are sick and throwing up around the house and you want to run to your room and lock the door and hide away, but instead you hug them and rub their back and pray over them. All these are ways that we as moms die to ourselves and serve our family in Christ. When we serve them in Christ's love, we are serving Him. People often ask me, "How do you get your kids to love God and serve Him?" The only answer I can think of is this: love God for yourself every day and your kids will follow you. "Follow my example, as I follow the example of Christ" (1 Corinthians 11:1).

I invite you to pray this prayer today:

Dear Heavenly Father,
Fill me with Your Holy Spirit and help me to make decisions that are in obedience to You. I pray that I would follow Jesus to the cross every day of my life and that through my example, my kids would learn to do the same. I love You Lord!
In Jesus' name, Amen.

DAY 58

Every Nation and Tribe

After this I looked, and there before me was a great multitude that no one could count, from every nation, tribe, people and language, standing before the throne and before the Lamb. They were wearing white robes and were holding palm branches in their hands. And they cried out in a loud voice: "Salvation belongs to our God, who sits on the throne, and to the Lamb."

REVELATION 7:9-10

It is so awesome how the Lord intentionally created various ethnicities and cultures and He loves our differences! This is something that is so important to teach our kids about from a young age. God purposed for each of us to be different and if we celebrate these differences in our families, our kids will learn to appreciate this about our world.

Celebrating cultures that differ from our own is an important step in understanding the heart of God in a deeper way. In heaven, we will be worshipping alongside our brothers and sisters of every skin color and every language and that is a beautiful thing. Since we will be together in heaven, why not teach out kids to love other cultures now?

There are gifts in each culture that God wants us to learn from. As moms, it takes intention and thought to introduce our kids to other ethnicities and cultures but I have found this to be a valuable part of parenting. One simple way you can start this is by exploring cuisines from different cultures. I am so thankful that the Unites States offers many opportunities for this. Our family has tried Turkish, Cuban, Mexican, Greek, Italian, Vietnamese, Spanish, Chinese, Japanese, Indian, Thai, Taiwanese, and many other foods, and I hope we can try even more! I absolutely love it when people of other ethnicities tell me that they enjoy Korean food because this is part of me. I grew up eating Korean food every day as a child growing up in the United States. Another way you can learn about other cultures is to invite people of different ethnicities into your home and become friends. Friendship is a beautiful way to build cultural bridges and deeper love and understanding.

I think something that will combat racism in our generation and the future generations is learning about God's heart for every nation of the world. I believe the Body of Christ should lead the way in building bridges between cultures and demonstrating God's love in this way.

I invite you to pray this prayer today:

Dear Heavenly Father,
Thank You for purposely creating us with differences. Please help me to honor Your creation and appreciate all of the distinct ways You made each person and people group. Help me to love the beauty of Your creation in every person that has been created in Your beautiful image. Please help me to teach my kids to love our many differences as well.
In Jesus' name, Amen.

DAY 59

Walk In Faith

And without faith it is impossible to please God, because anyone who comes to him must believe that he exists and that he rewards those who earnestly seek him.

HEBREWS 11:6

(I love this entire chapter in Hebrews, so if you have time today, please go and read the whole chapter.)

My Korean middle name is "Shinhaeng" which means "walk in faith." I don't know exactly why my parents chose this name, but I wonder if it was because they had to walk in faith and courage in order to have me. My parents immigrated to the United States over fifty years ago with three hundred dollars in their pocket, very few connections, and three little girls in tow under the age of five. My parents were not planning to have any more children, and they took measures to prevent future pregnancies, but they somehow got unexpectedly pregnant with me right after they landed here. We don't know if it was a miracle or if the medical procedure didn't work, but their doctor counseled them to abort me.

The Korean American doctor's reasoning was that my parents were very poor at the time, and God forbid that they have another girl! (In our Korean culture, having multiple girls at that time was considered a curse.) But my parents are strong Christians and they believed that God would take care of our family. They refused to have an abortion and chose to have me. Their courageous step of faith in the midst of great poverty and uncertainty altered the course of not only my life, but Chris' and my kids' lives as well.

Where the devil wants to bring death and destruction to your family, God wants to bring everlasting life and great fruitfulness. He wants us to thrive even in the midst of darkness and in Jesus, this is indeed possible!

I thank God for the deep faith that my parents imparted to me and that choosing God first will always trump the schemes of the devil against your life if you trust and obey Him. I believe one of my callings is to activate faith in the Body of Christ. Is there an area of faith in your family that God is inviting you into? If God is bringing something to your mind right now, trust Him my friends. Pursue Him with all of your heart and He will make a way if you grab hold of faith and courage and take another step forward towards that seemingly impossible God dream.

I invite you to pray this prayer today:

Dear Heavenly Father,
Please give me courage to walk forward in the dreams You have planted in my heart. Give me the faith to endure even when this step of faith is tested. I choose faith over fear for me and my family today.
In Jesus' name, Amen.

DAY 60

His Beautiful Bride

Then I saw "a new heaven and a new earth," for the first heaven and the first earth had passed away, and there was no longer any sea. I saw the Holy City, the new Jerusalem, coming down out of heaven from God, prepared as a bride beautifully dressed for her husband. And I heard a loud voice from the throne saying, "Look! God's dwelling place is now among the people, and he will dwell with them. They will be his people, and God himself will be with them and be their God. 'He will wipe every tear from their eyes. There will be no more death' or mourning or crying or pain, for the old order of things has passed away."

REVELATION 21:1-4

God's love is amazing. We are His bride, and He invites us into His heart and story. God is so much kinder than any of us realize and that is an incredible gift. To have a God who loves us and understands what it means to be human and live on this earth is incredible.

God gave me a short vision once of His bride getting ready on her wedding day. She looked radiant in her beautiful white wedding gown. As she started walking down the church aisle to her groom, all these people jumped on the back of her gown train. They had buckets of popcorn and were eating, like spectators do watching a movie. They were content to just sit back and watch what was happening, instead of getting ready themselves as Jesus' bride. The Lord asked me, "Eunice, will you be a bride getting ready for Jesus, her beloved Bridegroom, or will you be unprepared and content as a spectator just watching the scene unfolding before you?" It reminded me of the parable of the virgins in Matthew 25. Please go read it when you have time. The five foolish virgins were unprepared and did not have enough oil when the long-awaited Bridegroom finally arrived.

It is an honor and privilege to be preparing for Jesus' return as his bride. I believe that God has called me to encourage other moms to prepare ourselves and our children to prepare for His coming. No one knows when He is coming, but the Bible tells us, He is indeed coming back soon.

I hope that this devotional has strengthened you in your motherhood journey. I am praying that you will catch a new, fresh vision for motherhood from this book. God loves you and your children. He is inviting you to have a deeper vision into your high calling as a mother. You are forming world changers in your home. God believes in you and so do I.

Love and Blessings,
Eunice

ABOUT THE AUTHOR

Eunice Ho is passionate about encouraging the body of Christ in the areas of motherhood and marriage, the gift of prophecy, and overseas ministry. She has been married to Chris for twenty-one years and has been working alongside of him in ministry all of these years. Eunice is a mother of five (ranging from ages twenty to ten years old) and has homeschooled each of their kids at various points in their education. In 2020, Chris and Eunice founded The Journey Home Ministries. She is a podcaster, author, and speaker. You can find out more or connect with Eunice at:

thejourneyhome.global
Facebook.com/thejourneyhome.global
Instagram.com/thejourneyhome.global
Youtube.com/@thejourneyhome.global
euniceho@thejourneyhome.global

Made in United States
Orlando, FL
13 May 2023

33100880R00085